Greening The Garden

A Guide To Sustainable Growing

Dan Jason

Illustrated by Elaine Phillips

NEW SOCIETY PUBLISHERS
Philadelphia, PA   Santa Cruz, CA
Gabriola Island, BC

Canadian Cataloguing in Publication Data
Jason, Dan.
      Greening the garden

Includes bibliographical references.
ISBN 1-55092-170-3 (bound). — ISBN 1-55092-171-1 (pbk.)
         1. Organic gardening. 2. Vegetarianism.
I. Title.
SB453.5.J38 1991   635'.0484 C91-091412-5

Inquiries regarding requests to reprint all or part of *Greening the
Garden* should be addressed to:
New Society Publishers
4527 Springfield Avenue, Philadelphia, PA, USA 19143,
or
P.O. Box 189, Gabriola Island, BC, Canada V0R 1X0.

ISBN Canada   1-55092-170-3 Hardback
ISBN Canada   1-55092-171-1 Paperback
ISBN USA   0-86571-226-3 Hardback
ISBN USA   0-86571-227-1 Paperback

Cover art and design by Elaine Phillips.
Book design & typesetting by WebWorks, Salt Spring Island.

New Society Publishers is a project of the New Society Educational Foundation,
a non-profit, tax-exempt public foundation in the U.S.A., and the Catalyst
Education Society, a non-profit society registered in Canada. Opinions ex-
pressed in this book do not necessarily represent positions of the New Society
Educational Foundation, nor of the Catalyst Education Society.

Acknowledgments

Much of the material in this book has appeared in various magazines. I wish especially to acknowledge, for both their vision and editorial skills, Phyllis Kusch of *The Island Grower*, Heather Apple of the Heritage Seed Program, Sheila Harrington of *Positive Vibrations* and Jennifer Bennett of *Harrowsmith*.

I have been most fortunate to farm and garden with people who have a deep love for plants, animals and the land. Heartfelt thanks to Ross McLeod, Scott Kreisler, Marcus Knox, Darren Hearsey, John Wilcox, Naren Kartar and Brian Hutchings for their ongoing support, inspiration, expertise and camaraderie. I look forward to future projects and growings with all of them.

Tom Perry, a close friend for 20 years, unfortunately didn't live to see *Greening the Garden* published. His enthusiastic encouragement and perceptive criticism were invaluable contributions.

My richest exchange of gardening ideas, one which has been transpiring for over two decades, has been with Peter Light. I am particularly indebted to Peter for the section on mulching.

Important comments and perspectives came from Rosalie Bird, John William and John Wilcox.

Penny Hall magically, lovingly and so professionally transformed a collection of articles written for gardeners into an integrated book accessible to everyone.

Many thanks to Chris and Judith Plant for directing the publishing process so smoothly and efficiently.

Special thanks to my brother, Mike, for making Salt Spring Seeds an even more joyful operation, to my mother, Sally, for her unceasing faith in me, and to my children, Zama, Leif and Naomi, who teach me more than anyone about growing.

Table of Contents

Publisher's Note

How does a publisher of books that focus on social change through nonviolent action justify publishing a *gardening* book?

That was a question we asked ourselves when we considered whether or not New Society Publishers should publish this book. As keen gardeners who knew of his pioneering work with beans and odd South American plants, we anticipated liking what Dan Jason had produced. But, despite its being nonviolent, of course, we thought the chances of its being appropriate were slim.

When we perused it, however, we were delighted. And our delight grew when, having passed it on to a decidedly urban, non-gardener colleague to read, he came back with the enthusiastic comment that *this* book made him want to get out into the garden and start work! He was thoroughly inspired at having found a rare creature indeed: a book that made gardening a *political* act!

It's true. Much as *Greening the Garden* will be enjoyed because of the sheer wealth of information it contains for those who ordinarily have no trouble getting their hands into the earth, it also transforms gardening into an act of personal, political significance. As such it attracts even the most cerebral of non-gardeners. For example, if you personally want to contribute to making agriculture more sustainable, read this book and put its suggestions into practice. And if you want to break the agribusiness, meat and dairy monopolies, grow the new crops recommended here. Right now, in your own backyard, patio, or city allotment, you can actually contribute to a better diet for yourself, and a healthier planet as a consequence.

Greening the Garden is bioregionalism in practice. From the "How To" ideas for making compost or winter gardens, through the importance of saving and generating seed, and the philosophy toward nature that inform Dan's whole approach to gardening, this book inspires you to be thoroughly grounded, to translate your grief at how the world might be turning into practical acts to help sustain yourself and the Earth.

As we planted a variety of Dan's different beans this year, we couldn't help thinking of his wry humor and the obvious joy he exhibited while showing us the numerous shelves of glass, gallon jars of multi-colored bean varieties at his home. He'd like nothing better than for everyone to be raising them, living better and more sustainably as a result. — Gardening as politics; as therapy; as a subversive activity!

Christopher & Judith Plant
for New Society Publishers
June, 1991

Foreword

Good books on gardening abound. Here is another good one. I want to keep it at my elbow throughout my Maine gardening year.

Not only does this book give careful detailed means of preparing and sustaining a healthy productive soil and of enhancing soil fecundity by organic methods:

It is a good humored book about humus;

It itemizes special foods for essential nutriments;

It specifies certain weeds and wild plants (like chickweed and lamb's-quarters and dandelions) for nutritious food and simple safe medicines;

It digs new ground in systems and uses of winter gardening;

It is a happy book giving happy methods of achieving happy health;

It feeds the soul with inspired dithyrambs on why gardeners are luckier than most people, benefiting physically, emotionally, artistically and spiritually from their work on the land.

Good husbandry is enhanced through the reading of this book. Go to it, and green your garden!

Helen K. Nearing
Harborside, Maine
April, 1991

Introduction

There seems to be no end to gardening books, so you may well ask, "Why another one?" Like many such books, this one is about growing good food well, but is different in that it places food growing in the context of our current environmental dilemma.

Certainly all of us have an intimate connection with the environment two or three times a day—when we *eat* parts of it. Yet, despite daily reports of ozone depletion, global warming and pollution, to name a few, we rarely hear about how our food systems and choices impact on the earth. So, whether you're a gardener, a would-be gardener, or just plain interested in your health and that of the planet, *Greening the Garden* offers you practical advice on techniques and food choices that can help restore environmental balance.

People are increasingly seeking food that is grown without chemicals and poisons. Part One of this book discusses ways of growing food that are ecologically sound—methods that have long been embraced by proponents of organic gardening. Part Two presents many plants

1

whose capacity to nourish and sustain us is far greater than those we currently grow in North America. Mass popularization of some of these crops would begin to reverse the harm caused by our current choices in food production. Part Three offers perspectives on our food system within the global context. It encourages us not only to choose and grow foods more wisely, but also to consider everyone's right to do the same. In our global village, it has become all too evident that exploiting other peoples' gardens impoverishes our own. The best way to ensure a planet where our children, as adults, will enjoy at least as varied and as wholesome a bounty as they do now, is to move towards fulfilling our needs locally.

This book is addressed to gardeners right across Canada and the United States. Although all my gardening experience has been on the west coast of British Columbia where winters are mild and summers are cool, there are only a few subjects that don't have general relevance. Winter gardening is largely a coastal or southern celebration and only a few of the overwintering vegetables I describe will make it through a winter harsher than this maritime one. Some of the plants presented in the chapter on weeds might be unfamiliar to some people. As well, quinoa is a crop very new to North America and it is still not certain if it can be grown successfully in areas with very hot summers. But the rest of the crops and all the growing techniques should work in your gardens—no matter where you live—as well as they do in mine.

Gardening is by far the most popular leisure-time activity in North America. Some 75 million of us spend time and money caring for the bit of nature surrounding our homes. It is the underlying theme of this book that by acting locally and committing ourselves to the greening opportunities in our gardens, we will help to restore economic and ecological balance on a planetary scale.

The terms "green" and "sustainable" have become catchwords in the past few years and have not been used in the context of food gardens before. They might seem awkward at first, but what is a garden, if not green? And what is food, if not something that sustains us? The deep-rooted meaning of "green" has blossomed fully to connote a certain social and environmental awareness. On the other hand, "sustainable" is a seedling from a new catalogue of perennials. The term "sustainable development" was popularized in 1987 by the United Nations' Commission on Environment and Development, otherwise known as the Brundtland Commission. The commission intended to foster the idea that development must meet current needs and, in recognition of the interrelatedness of all systems within the environment, must also focus on preserving our resources—soil, water, air, plant and animal life—for future generations. The pairing of "development" with "sustainable" is a most unfortunate and inappropriate one for it implies that some kinds of growth can go on forever, that we can continue to take from earth's bounty with no thought of return. And in spite of the way the words "green" and "sustainable" have been tattooed into our consciousness by the media, they are still potent words. The yearning for a whole and healthy planet that they represent is increasingly universal.

Nations that have pursued the path of endless increase now face ecological problems that seem insurmountable. Yet if, in our daily actions, each of us takes the environment fully into account, sustainability can become a reality. What this requires is a new way of thinking about our relationship to nature. To be truly nourished by our gardens' abundance requires circular, rather than linear movement: an attitude of taking and giving inspired by the delicate balance in which all the planet's systems and lifeforms coexist. Both "green" and "sustainable" speak of an ability and a dedication to grow foods forever on the same patch of earth; they represent a nostalgia for the future, a longing for a way of being on this planet that supports and nourishes its integrity, and ultimately our own.

Sustainability is inherent in green gardening. The concept reflects my desire to articulate a particular ethos, spirit and politics of gardening towards which I've been growing for many years. I don't imagine I'll ever arrive at a "destination," for I conceptualize our movement towards sustainable living as a process that comes from ongoing knowledge and self-realization and which never really ends. Many years from now, I expect to echo the words of Thomas Jefferson: "I may be an old man, but I'm still a young gardener."

Part One

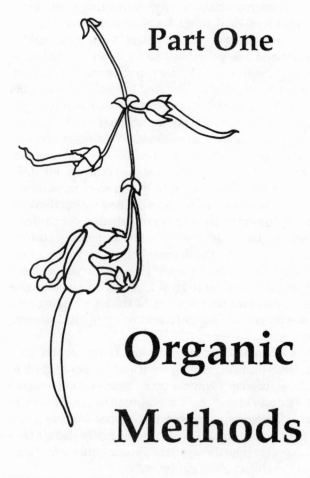

Organic
Methods

Chemical-based food growing practices have been pervasive in North America since the '50s. The results? Pesticide use has increased tenfold, yet crop loss due to pests has nearly doubled. Topsoil erosion, water degradation and food contamination have reached horrendous levels.

Chemical farming is now being seen for what it is: a quick-fix approach that looks good at first, but has serious and dangerous consequences. The long-standing debate about the quality of non-organic versus organic food has obscured an essential point. It is the health and viability of the soil that is of paramount importance. Plants grown with chemical fertilizers will likely yield good food at first, given good soil to start with. But growing food year after year with only chemical boosters and biocides impoverishes the soil and results ultimately in striking deterioration in food quality. Likewise, soil that is poor to start with won't grow abundant, high-quality food with organic methods until the land has been well-managed for some years.

We can continue to set ourselves apart as humans and to lord it over nature only to our imminent demise. No matter how sophisticated our technology, a sick earth can't grow healthy people.

With the increasing need to authenticate organic food in the market place, what constitutes "organic" has become a hotly debated issue. This first section touches some of that debate but mostly presents the organic philosophy as the down-to-earth approach that it is. The home gardener passes the preliminary organic certification test if growing food is more a matter of love than of formulae, is a celebration rather than a sacrifice, is a dance and a communion rather than a contest or battle.

Organic methods are testaments to mindfulness rather than reactive impositions of will. A short example is a case in point. No insect in North America has been subjected to greater all-out pesticide assault than the cotton boll weevil of the southeastern United States. Not only have all the highly touted insecticides of the post-World War II era failed to stop the weevil, they have caused additional problems by wiping out predatory and parasitic insects, thus releasing a host of new pests on the cotton crop. Ironically, as early as 1896, a U.S. Department of Agriculture publication described an effective technique for dealing with the weevil. Each year, the summer's last generation of weevils seek a winter haven in standing cotton stalks, allowing a substantial population of them to get a head start on the new crop in the spring. It wasn't until the late 1980s that the simple, "organic" tactic of shredding and plowing under cotton stalks after harvest was tried throughout Texas—and with far greater success than chemical warfare.

The above example is illustrative of the kind of awareness advocated by the organic philosophy. Attuning to natural processes enables us to honor and work with them and to be mindful of some basic questions: "What do my plants need?" "Where does what I use in the garden come from?" "What costs are incurred in getting it to me?" "Are there healthier alternatives?" The organic methods described in this section are the nearest-to-hand, most sustainable ones. They simplify the first questions with their happy alternative.

1

Organic Growing For Sustainability

The organic movement is finally coming of age. People want to eat food that is as safe and nutritious as the food served on farm tables in days gone by. Well-managed farms growing diverse crops without chemicals are proving just as productive and often more profitable than those using chemicals. The demand for organic food is currently much greater than the supply. Farmers and gardeners everywhere are responding to this demand, taking a "giant step back to the future" and turning to sustainability by switching to organic techniques.

Reversing Past Practices

Certainly the first step in going organic is to stop using chemical weed killers and bug killers. Nearly 500 insects and 50 types of weeds have now developed immunity to biocides. Pesticides, herbicides and fungicides are a hazard to us and our environment and cause more problems than they attempt to solve. The desire to create the cosmetically perfect landscape has inadvertently turned many of our backyards into toxic sites that are inhospitable to wildlife, pets and children, not to mention ourselves.

The second step is to stop using synthetic fertilizers. It is generally known that they do not benefit the soil, but the harm that they do is only now being widely recognized. Chemical fertilizers dissolve quickly in water, rapidly increasing the levels of nitrate, phosphate and potassium available to plants. This is the seemingly desired effect. As they do this, however, they impede the activity of soil organisms that make nitrogen and phosphorous more gradually available to plants over time and they inhibit the absorption of the elements calcium and magnesium which are essential to plant health. The net result is soft, abundant top growth and reduced soil fertility. The lush growth looks more appetizing, and indeed it is, to a host of pests. As well, the imbalance of growth makes plants more disease-prone. Soils also become more acidic with the addition of synthetic fertilizers. This acidity repels beneficial earthworms and changes soil structure by dissolving the material that cements soil particles together. Rivers and lakes also become more acidic as soluble fertilizers leach into them.

The Nature of Organic Growing

Organic gardening has been defined as "growing without the use of chemical pesticides and artificial fertilizers." This is only a partial description, however, which implies that organic growers leave their gardens and fields to nature. Rather, organic growers use many techniques in order to work as closely as possible with nature. The main aim is to create a healthy, balanced environment and to renounce the mode of thinking wherein every insect is a pest, every uncultivated plant a weed, and the solution to every problem, a spray.

Organic growing is a process of attunement that calls for looking at and responding to the whole ecosystem in which plants are growing, rather than concentrating on isolated aspects. Modern science has confirmed what non-technological societies have always known: that the vitality of any system is maintained by the interaction of all its parts.

Organic gardeners employ a wide range of methods and materials aimed at soil care. In fact, their central maxim is "feed the soil." Soil is the on-going result or function of a whole living environment, not simply "the stuff that keeps the plants upright." Organic soil additions aim to feed the entire spectrum of soil life, from worms to microscopic bacteria, whose activities release food for plants gradually, in balanced form.

A fertile soil not only contains such plant foods in appropriate sufficiency but also has a compositional structure that provides the living conditions suitable to both soil organisms and plant roots. To maintain the structure and fertility of the soil, organic growers grow cover crops and green manures and apply animal manures, mulches, seaweed and compost. These strategies all require knowledge and expertise and go hand in hand with soil testing and cultivation practices for maximum soil benefit. For example, tractors and tillers are not operated when they might unnecessarily compact the soil.

On the other hand, there are also organic products designed specifically to feed plants rather than the soil. Bonemeal, dried blood, kelp meal, fish meal and rock phosphate are common organic fertilizers. They differ from artificial fertilizers in that they need to break down in the soil before they become available to plants.

The main thrust of pest and disease management for organic growers is to create the healthy soil and balanced environment that will produce strong vigorous plant growth and deter outbreaks of pests and diseases in the first place. They also plant a wide range of crops so that disease or insect damage to one variety is not calamitous. But organic practitioners also employ strategies to maintain healthy plants. They pick off bugs and remove diseased plant parts by hand. They use mechanical protections, such as barriers around brassica plants to ward off the cabbage root fly; mini-greenhouses (sometimes called cloches) to keep slugs and snails away from young plants; and timely sowings to take advantage of insect cycles. Biological controls for pests, such as parasitic wasps, predatory mites, *Trichoderma* fungus and *Bacillus thuringensis*, cause minimal harm to the environment. Because rhubarb and garlic generally repel bugs, sprays made from these plants usually help protect more vulnerable plants.

In nature there are rarely great pest and disease problems; every creature has its place and is kept there by the interplay of other species. The more diverse a garden the more likely it is to attract the wide range of organisms that will maintain a dynamic balance by their own nature. The organic gardener often encourages natural controls by providing a large range of habitats and food plants in the garden. This may be done by providing nesting sites to attract birds, planting native trees, shrubs and hedges, leaving patches of long grass or weedy areas as protective covers, growing specific plants to attract beneficial insects or making a small pond as a home for frogs and toads. Identifying a pest or disease and learning about its habits and life cycle are fascinating avocations that help the gardener decide whether the problem really merits action and prevent the killing of beneficial insects and plants.

The organic grower's aim is not the eradication of any species, but a willingness to live in harmony with the fluctuating balance that is inherent in any life system. The organic philosophy respects the life-giving properties of food rather than the dubious aesthetics of perfection. Occasional bites or blemishes on fruit, leaf or root don't cause the organic gardener to throw arms up in despair and throw away the food as unacceptable.

The organic grower prefers to keep weeds under control, rather than to eliminate them entirely. There are no organic weed killers but there are a variety of control methods beyond hoeing, hand weeding and rototilling. Thick, light-excluding mulches will suppress and eventually kill the majority of weeds. Green manures inhibit weed growth as well. Vegetables grown in blocks at close spacing will need far less weeding than those in conventional rows. Another technique is letting the first flush of weeds appear in a prepared bed and cleaning it before sowing the intended crop.

The organic approach to growing food demands a little more time and work than the quick-fix one whereby long-range costs are ignored. The organic gardener considers this exercise and study to be joyful and dignified activities that bring greater understanding of and respect for natural processes. Underlying the organic approach is the belief that we are not separate from the food we eat nor from the soil it grows in. Soil is not something to be owned and mined. We belong to it as much as earthworms or bean plants do. In effect, we borrow our lives from it.

Organic *and* Sustainable

In September 1989, the U.S. National Academy of Sciences issued a landmark study advocating a national policy shift to organic farming. The U.S. Organic Foods Production Act of 1990, a result of this study, will greatly change the way Americans grow food. By necessity, organic growing—once a vague concept—is becoming more precisely defined. Federal, state and provincial governments in both Canada and the U.S. are presently debating standards by which foods can be labelled "organic" and implementing certification programs for organic growers. "Sustainable" crops up in most of these discussions as a word which helps to define "organic"—usually in the context of growing practices that are intended to achieve "sustainable" productivity. However, what is meant by "sustainable" itself seems quite vague and nebulous in definitions of "organic" I've seen so far.

For me, the concept of sustainability implies more than safe food-growing practices that maximize the soil's inherent fertility. Sustainable growing does not exhaust the resources of any given place and moves towards independence from those external inputs that require reliance on someone else's system. Thus, in my opinion, an organic garden is not necessarily a sustainable one. I have always used "organic" methods and principles. They are good and I would not do otherwise. Yet for me, the concept of sustainability moves organic gardening to a deeper level of awareness.

Take, for instance, the example of corn, which is a heavy feeder. It is difficult to maintain soil fertility in corn patches using only traditional organic methods, such as composting and cover cropping. Growing lots of corn year after year usually means dependence on relatively high levels of fertilizer from outside the garden. Having to obtain fertilizer, even if it is "organic," could represent either a sustainable or a non-sustainable practice. Buying manure from cattle feedlots, for example, carries a greater environmental debt than would getting it from your neighbor. Seaweed may be available from a nearby harbor, but excessive gathering can destroy a fragile ecosystem. Bonemeal, bloodmeal and cottonseed meal may sound like wonderful organic fertilizers. However, as their names imply, bonemeal and bloodmeal generally come from animals, some of which are diseased; most are raised in conditions that are ecologically destructive. Cottonseed meal comes from the cotton plant, the most pesticide-ridden crop in North America.

On a broader scale, there are few organic farmers or gardeners who are ready to relinquish dependence on petrochemicals to power machinery and to deliver goods and services. Yet, it is possible to make choices that lessen reliance on non-renewable resources. A rototiller can be a more appropriate tool than a tractor and a walking hand-cultivator can often serve better than a rototiller. A locally-produced soil amendment may be the best "buy" when the fact that it didn't have to be transported thousands of miles to your garden is taken into account.

All things considered, I now find myself re-evaluating some of my previous choices in terms of sustainability. This book does not focus on the tools and products that maintain the grower's status as consumer, but rather on ways and means for the gardener to become a food producer in conjunction with nature. The next two chapters are about traditional soil enhancement methods that support the self-contained and self-perpetuating garden.

Clearly, organic gardening is not as short-sighted an approach as the chemical methods that give little thought to contemporary creatures or to future generations. The term "sustainable gardening" encompasses organic growing methods but also places them in a context of interpersonal commitment and global responsibility. Sustainable gardening goes beyond the insular notion of a home garden to a vision that values all living communities or ecosystems on the planet—the health of each fostering the health of all. Both organic gardening and sustainable gardening might be considered metaphors for human participation with, rather than mastery over, nature. The concept of sustainable gardening has further value for me in that, in such a context, one can answer the question, "Sustainable for whom?" with the response, "Sustainable for all."

2

Composting:
An Organic Fundamental

Composting is the foundation of organic gardening and a crucial part of growing green. It is a superior way to enrich and revitalize the soil and it recycles organic matter and nutrients that would otherwise be hauled off to landfills or burned in incinerators.

Making your own compost is a magical act. You bring together mouldy bread, apple cores, grass clippings, salad trimmings, leaves, straw, egg shells and wood ashes, and it all becomes rich dark brown, sweet-smelling earth. You make some garden beds, add your fresh compost to them and plant some seeds in the humus you've helped create. The plants that grow there are free of disease and pests and they are the most vibrant you've ever seen.

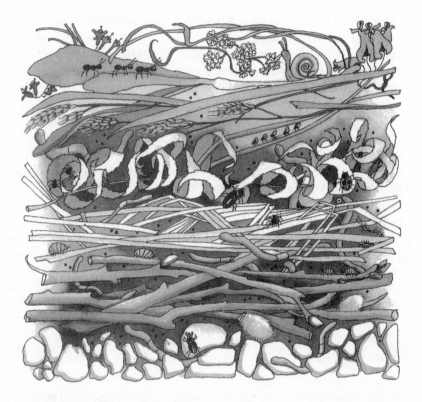

What is Compost?

You'll find the spongy and moist, dark brown or black substance called humus on any forest floor. When plants and creatures die, they are consumed by billions of soil organisms and reduced to their elemental ingredients with no hint of their original form. Humus not only embodies the endless cycle of birth, death and renewal; it is the lifeblood of productive soil. It makes the difference between eroded, burned-out wasteland and flourishing forest, farm, garden or orchard where varied biological systems thrive in balance.

The only difference between a gardener's finished compost and humus found in the forest is the time it takes to produce them—on the average, three to six months for compost and 500 to 1000 years for an inch of forest topsoil. Here's how it works. When appropriate materials are gathered together in a loose heap, microorganisms, such as bacteria, fungi, actinomycetes and algae start to feed on the softer, more succulent parts. Their numbers increase rapidly as does the rate of decomposition. (A mere gram of humus-rich soil contains several billion bacteria, about a million fungi, ten to twenty million actinomycetes and up to a million algae!) If the heap is large enough to build the heat from all the activity, the temperature can reach 160°F (70°C)—hot enough to deactivate weed seeds plus reduce levels of plant pathogens and toxic substances. Once the tender material is consumed, the compost pile cools and allows larger decomposers such as earthworms, beetles and centipedes to move in. (Another amazing statistic: earthworm castings are three times richer in nitrogen, twice as rich in exchangeable calcium, seven times richer in available phosphorous and eleven times richer in available potassium than the soil they process.) By the end of the process, most of the original ingredients will have been broken down, mixed together and rebuilt into dark, rich-looking, crumbly compost. A carefully-tended pile of well-prepared materials can be used as compost in just a few weeks.

The Process

You don't have to be a particularly knowledgeable or dedicated gardener to make your own compost and there are numerous ways to go about it. All the gardener or humus maker does is to help speed along the natural process by which organic materials break down. The aim is to provide air, moisture and suitable food in the right proportions to keep the beneficial organisms functioning as desired. Most compost materials are either kitchen wastes or garden debris. Composting success depends on mixing the right combination of these, allowing air to get at the compost and keeping the pile moist but not soggy. If there is too much moisture and insufficient air, different organisms take over and anaerobic (without oxygen) decomposition takes place—a process which is slower, smellier and which doesn't produce much heat. If materials are too dry, decomposition will be very slow. However, compost piles are very forgiving: whatever your style or method, they always reward your efforts.

What to Use

The type of organic waste you use to build your compost heap is largely determined by available materials. Most kitchen wastes and leftovers, whether raw or cooked, are ideal. Meat and bones however are likely to attract rats and other animals, and fats, grease and oils are as hard for microbes to digest as they are for humans. Animal manures from farm animals make excellent additions to compost. You can add seaweed, algae, sods, sawdust (preferably weathered), egg shells, coffee grounds, straw, hay, weeds, wood ashes, pulverized nuts and sea shells, as well as chopped plant stalks and leaves. The smaller the compost materials, the faster the composting process. The more kinds of ingredients the better. Green matter has abundant moisture and nitrogen and breaks down rapidly, but a pile made mostly from grass clippings or leaves may become very soggy. Absorbent but dry weathered material balances out fresh vegetable or garden matter and provides better ventilation.

It is usually easiest and most efficient to build a compost pile in more or less equal layers, alternating dry materials that are high in carbon, such as straw, sawdust and corn stalks, with green, high-nitrogen materials, such as grass clippings, manure and vegetable trimmings. A good rule of thumb is to avoid layers more than six inches (15 cm) thick of any one material.

Tips for Success

There are myriad ways to build a compost pile. I usually begin by choosing a sunny, airy, accessible location away from standing water. Then I loosen the soil on my chosen site to a depth of a foot (30 cm) or more to provide good drainage and expose the bottom layer to soil organisms. Next, I lay down about six inches (15 cm) of roughage to ensure a good flow of air into the pile. Plant stalks, miscellaneous brush cuttings and prunings can be used. (A nearby stand of quick-growing Jerusalem artichokes is excellent for this purpose.) I then put down a layer of dry matter such as straw, leaves, old garden waste or hay and on top of that a few inches of green vegetation and kitchen waste. (I frequently use leaves from my nearby comfrey patch and kitchen wastes fill a bucket under our kitchen sink every three or four days.) Next, I lightly cover these first layers with soil and/or wood ashes to detract flies and prevent odors. The pile is built to shoulder height by adding new layers of dry vegetation, green vegetation, kitchen waste and soil as these materials become available.

A minimum volume of three cubic feet (four in cold climates) is needed to properly insulate the heat of the composting process but in the end it will shrink to less than half this mass. I water the pile whenever necessary to keep everything wet but not soggy. ("Soggy" being if I could squeeze water from a handful.) In unusually wet weather, I sometimes cover the pile with burlap to keep it from becoming too moist.

Using my favorite digging fork, I turn the mixture every week or two and bring the outer parts to the centre. I try to maintain an adjacent open space to facilitate this task. If the particle sizes I've added are small, the weather warm and if I turn my pile as often as every few days, I get good compost in about three weeks. More often my compost piles are ready in two to six months.

Rather than let it deteriorate, I add finished compost to the garden, spreading it an inch or more thick on beds and around plantings or mixing it into the soil with my fork. I also screen it to use in potting mixes or to provide an especially fine soil surface. Mature compost smells good, crumbles in your hands and has few discernible remains of original ingredients.

More Helpful Hints

Composting in the above manner takes approximately equal amounts by weight of dry vegetation, fresh wastes and soil. A lot of composting recipes recommend natural "activators" to help start and maintain fermentation in the heap. These include alfalfa meal, animal manures and matured compost. I add thin layers of these if available but I find that ordinary soil contains an adequate starter supply of microorganisms. I also favor comfrey and nettle leaves to help get the bacterial bonfire going.

Some composters add material as available and some collect material beside the compost site until there is enough to make a three or four cubic foot heap all at once. Some composters don't turn their pile, some turn it once with a fork, some turn it often with a shovel. (Turning a pile is great exercise or hard work depending on who is doing it!) To increase aeration and speed decomposition, some composters stand perforated pipes in the middle as they're building their compost; others plunge composting wands, pipes or wooden stakes through the completed pile, then wiggle and jiggle them.

A compost pile needn't be contained but usually it is neater, more efficient and manageable to enclose the operation. Again, whatever works is fine and most anything works.

Many gardening centres sell a variety of composting units. For those with the time and energy to make their own, possibilities abound. On the smallest scale, a barrel, wooden box or large garbage can with the lid knocked out and holes in the sides might serve to begin composting. Home-made holding bins can be wood and wire units, four wooden pallets nailed together or a circular standing wire mesh unit. These "holding" apparati, however, do not allow easy turning of the materials. Bins that permit turning of the compost are more efficient and can easily be constructed out of cinder blocks, wood, bricks or chicken wire. Fast compost is often made in a series of large bins with accessible sides that open for emptying. A fresh pile is built in the first unit, then mixed and turned into the second when the temperature of the pile falls; yet undigested material is moved to the centre of this second heap. A few weeks later the completed pile is turned into a third bin, ready to be used in the garden.

The Benefits

A compost program sustains garden soil in maximum health with little or no expense. It is almost impossible to overuse compost: the more you dig into your soil, the better. Compost improves the texture and structure of all soils, turning stodgy clay into friable loam and loose sand into retentive earth. The microbes that feed on soil humus continuously excrete a whole range of organic compounds. These bind soil particles together in a manner that ensures good aeration, drainage and water retention plus resistance to erosion. Even a small amount of compost spread over a garden has a beneficial inoculant effect on the soil due to the rapidity at which microorganisms multiply.

For Plants

There are other extremely valuable benefits of composting. Compost acts as a storehouse and natural timed-release dispenser of plant nutrients. Microorganisms in humus bind chemical elements and release them gradually as the plants need them. Synthetic chemicals aren't as versatile: once dissolved in the soil water, they are taken up by the plant roots in whatever combination they were added. Excessive concentrations of chemicals (which make plants susceptible to disease) are thus avoided by using humus-rich soil.

Compost harbors earthworms and beneficial fungi that fight nematodes and other soil pests. Recent studies have shown that plants grown in organically composted soil take up less lead and other pollutants. Compost contributes a high volume of top-quality organic matter to the soil without tying up garden space (as cover crops do) and it stabilizes soil pH at a neutral to slightly acid level—the ideal range for most vegetables. (The pH scale runs from 0, which is pure acid, to 14, which is pure lye. From the neutral point, 7, the numbers increase or decrease in geometric progression: thus, pH 5 is 10 times more acidic than pH 6, pH 4 is 100 times more acidic, etc.)

For the Planet

Composting is also an ecologically responsible activity. No matter what composting procedures one follows, precious resources are conserved rather than squandered in already overflowing garbage landfills. Careless agriculture and silviculture practices have depleted our life-supporting topsoil to the extent that we have already lost over 75% of this most precious resource. It can take 500 years for nature to build an inch of topsoil yet North American land is currently losing this inch every 16 years. With less than six inches (15 cm) of topsoil remaining, catastrophe is imminent.

About one third of our household garbage consists of organic materials that can be recycled back into the ground. People who don't have gardens can save compostable materials for friends and neighbors who do. Dedicated composters can approach stores and restaurants, local sawmills and park commissions for vast amounts of organic refuse that can be returned to the soil. Even at the home garden level, composting makes a strong contribution to regenerating and replenishing our earth.

Our throw-away mentality has come from an exaggerated sense of our own power over nature. Composting consciousness reveres the myriad life forms of the soil, bows low in the alchemical dance of earth, air, fire and water, and humbly yet proudly co-creates bounteous riches for life to come. The shepherding of compostable material means we shall not want. Composting is the ultimate in recycling: Earth provides our food, clothing and shelter and we close the circle by intensifying its fertility and health.

3

More Soil Enhancement

Cover cropping and mulching with organic materials are two additional methods of greening the garden. As with composting, their desirability stems from the fundamental organic principle of feeding the soil rather than the plant.

Most cover crops are grains or legumes grown primarily to be mixed directly back into the soil or to be cut down and composted. Cover cropping has been an agricultural tradition for centuries and home gardeners are now starting to realize its benefits. Mulching, on the other hand, is familiar to many gardeners. It involves placing materials on top of the soil where plants are or will be growing. Either technique can be used in small or large areas, throughout or in part of a garden. They cost very little, yet reap enormous benefits.

Both techniques feed the soil naturally with organic matter crucial for a vital, healthy, productive garden. They protect the surface layer of the soil, increasing the beneficial activity of bacteria, fungi and earthworms. At the same time they prevent soil from washing or blowing away, baking dry, or compacting under heavy rain. Both cover crops and mulches do an excellent job of suppressing weeds as well.

Cover Cropping

Cover crops, also known as green manures, have the potential to supply most, if not all, of your garden's nutritional needs. In many respects, they act as living mulches with benefits beyond the reach of normal, on-top-of-the-soil mulches. Research into cover cropping is increasingly popular, and the possibilities are very exciting.

Benefits

Green manures condition both clay and sandy soils, moderating either extreme (as do animal manures). Legumes especially will loosen compaction and add humus in heavy clay soils. Leguminous cover crops—clovers, alfalfa, vetches, peas and beans—can also provide a bonus of extra nitrogen in soil by "fixing" it from the air and storing it in nodules along their roots. In sandy soils, the bulky, deep roots of cereal crops draw up needed phosphorus, potassium and trace minerals that would otherwise be below the reach of most vegetable roots. The matted roots of cereal crops enable the soil to absorb more water. They keep plant foods locked up in their tissues until decay releases them for a succeeding crop.

Disadvantages

There are few disadvantages to growing cover crops. In a large space, turning over a green manure by hand is very labor-intensive. But a rototiller works wonders. The other main disadvantage applies to northern gardens where, during the growing season, cover crops take up space that could be producing lots of food.

Common Cover Crops

The most common cover crops are described below—some legumes, some grains. Most of these are available at farms or through garden centres. Merchants will also provide information on seeding rates, depths to cover seed, best varieties for your garden, best times to turn crops and whatever other questions you may have.

Legumes

Alfalfa is hard to establish unless your soil is well-drained and fairly neutral. It has deep roots and is a very productive nitrogen fixer. Alfalfa can be cut several times annually for mulch. A stand of alfalfa can last many years if not turned over.

Clovers tolerate much more humid and acidic conditions than alfalfa. Dutch white clover is low-growing and great as a living mulch. The biennial clover, Alsike, is the most tolerant of wet and acidic soils. Other clovers include Red, Sweet White and White Ladino, which prefer loamy soil, plus Crimson and Sweet Yellow, which are more adaptable.

Fava beans are widely adaptable, have low fertility needs, tolerate acidic soils and fix high amounts of nitrogen. They thrive under cool growing conditions and will normally survive a coastal winter if fall planted. When planted in the spring, they can produce a high protein summer crop. As with other edible legumes, their roots can be left in the ground at harvest time and the foliage can either be composted or mulched down on the spot and covered with hay, leaves or other mulch material.

Soybeans and other warm weather beans appreciate rich soil and are ideally planted in May or June to serve both as a food and as a cover crop.

The vetches tolerate a wide range of soils, have low fertility needs and high drought tolerance. Hairy vetch is the hardiest and is often overwintered with oats and rye. It prefers a well-drained soil.

Field peas fix the least nitrogen of the legumes. Austrian Winter pea thrives in cool, moist conditions, so is a popular winter cover crop on the west coast. It is a good weed competitor, especially when sown with oats.

Lupines have deep roots and make a dependable first crop in a rebuilding scheme. Large White lupine is the most winter-hardy.

Chick-peas or **garbanzo beans** are among the highest nitrogen fixers and are also a nutritious and delicious food. They can be sown as early as peas.

Planting **pea** and **bean varieties** intended for the table and turning the residue under after harvest is another way of having your cover crops and eating them too.

Grains

Winter rye tops the list of the best, non-legume winter cover crops. The seeds germinate in cool fall weather, the plants tolerate extremely cold temperatures and they resume growing in the spring to prevent topsoil erosion from heavy spring rains.

Barley prefers a neutral to alkaline pH and is highly drought-tolerant. It can be sown in fall or spring and turned under in spring or fall.

Buckwheat is an excellent soil-builder. With an early start, gardeners can turn under two or three crops a season, adding great amounts of organic matter to the soil. Buckwheat draws up phosphorous from deeper soil levels and is high in calcium. It will grow in poor soil and is miraculous at suppressing weeds. Its white flowers are much sought after by bees and it readily reseeds itself if not turned under. It will not tolerate frost, so should be planted from late spring onward.

Millet tolerates poor and dry acidic soils and should be sown in spring to be turned under in the fall.

Oats can be grown on a variety of soils but do best in cool, moist conditions. As a green manure planted in spring, it grows well with peas and beans. For a winter cover, oats should be planted early in fall since it dies after the first hard frost.

Annual ryegrass also dies in winter so it should be planted by late August to leave a thatch of stubby residue through till spring. Both ryegrass and oats allow crops to be planted earlier in spring than winter rye but they contribute less organic matter and are less of a deterrent to spring weeds.

Spring wheat is sown in the spring to be turned under in the fall and winter wheat is sown in the fall to be turned under in the spring. Both prefer a fertile, loamy, not-too-acidic soil, but both tolerate low-moisture conditions.

Rye and wheat both contain natural toxins which will suppress not only weed growth, but also insect pests in subsequent crops.

Further Considerations

After turning under a green manure, delay planting at least a week in the case of legumes and two weeks for grains. Early decomposition gives off ethylene gas which inhibits seed germination; also, multiplying microorganisms temporarily use up available nitrogen as they break down the green manure. Winter rye and winter barley also release toxins which can affect emerging veggies as well as weed seedlings. How long it takes the cover crop to decay sufficiently is directly related to how fibrous and mature it is when turned under. Most green manures are incorporated into the soil while they are still lush and green and therefore break down fairly fast. If they mature past this stage, plants start to consist of much more carbon than nitrogen. In this case, the addition of bloodmeal, composted manure or other nitrogen sources can speed up the decomposition process; as can a dusting of lime if your soil is on the acidic side.

Cover cropping is a very open-ended concept. Even if you have space for only two months, it's amazing how quickly cover crops like buckwheat and oats can grow. In certain places, even weeds can be allowed lush growth before turning them under if you're careful about not letting the most pernicious ones go to seed. In fact, the possibility of utilizing weeds as a green manure (or in the compost pile or as mulch) reflects the organic philosophy that proper management techniques can enhance the biological relevance of everything in the garden.

Complementary Techniques

Crop rotation and intercropping are refinements of cover cropping that involve more sophisticated and longer-range planning. Many cultures have relied successfully on these techniques to maintain soil fertility. Though they are somewhat more appropriate to larger scale growing, they can be used with much benefit in small gardens.

Crop Rotation

Crop rotation is the practice of alternating both cover crops and food plants on the same piece of ground. Developing a rotation scheme can extend the advantages of green manuring in many ways. Rotations further improve soil structure and increase soil nitrogen, bacterial activity and the release of carbon dioxide. They help keep pests in balance and discourage certain weeds from gaining a foothold, especially when repeated over several years. A sequence that includes deep-rooted food and cover crops extracts nutrients from layers of the soil not used by shallow rooters, leaves paths for the roots of less vigorous crops, and increases the depth of the topsoil.

There are many beneficial ways to rotate crops. A general principle is to avoid planting successive crops that are related botanically, that have common diseases or pests, or have the same soil requirements. This requires either experience or a little homework, but is well worth the effort.

Rotations can be sequential or overlapping. In either case, however, it helps to know what nutrients each crop takes from the soil as well as the fertilization and cultivation methods to which each responds. For instance, sweet corn, in contrast to most other crops, does well following any member of the brassica family. To take advantage of this, you could for example, sow a leguminous green manure under established cabbage, let it overlap the cabbage harvest, then turn it under the following spring to provide ideal growing conditions for sweet corn. Another example is to plant root crops after squash, which is known to benefit them. Also, since squash is easy to keep weed free, fewer weeds are likely in subsequent root crops, which are among the most difficult to keep cleanly cultivated.

Because of the pervasiveness of monoculture farming, where the same crop is grown in the same place year after year, research in crop rotation is scanty. Some studies have been done, however, on how crop rotation affects yields. They show that any given crop can affect the succeeding one, or be affected by the preceding one. For instance, onions, lettuces, squash and legumes help succeeding crops, but onions, themselves, are not benefited by a preceding legume. Potatoes yield highest after corn. Soybeans greatly decrease the incidence of scab in succeeding potato crops, whereas peas, oats and barley increase it. Carrots, beets and cabbage often reduce the yield in crops that follow them, but corn and beans are not affected negatively by the preceding crop.

Rotation schemes also take into account crop preferences for the timing of soil amendments, such as compost and animal manures. For instance, cabbages, tomatoes and root crops grow better on ground manured the previous year while corn and squash do well in ground manured the same year.

Basically crop rotation means variety, which gives stability to biological systems. The longer the rotation period before the same crop is grown again, the better. Many organic farmers practice five-year or even eight-year rotations, but even short rotations can be valuable in small-scale gardens. (Researchers are now fine-tuning shorter rotation sequences.) In any case, planning is necessary as many factors need to be taken into account in setting up the sequences. One example you might try is a two-year rotation: peas, then beans, then rye during the first year, followed in year two by a heavy feeder such as corn, and then another planting of rye. In each case all residues are returned to the soil. Another possibility is to have two simultaneous gardens—one for vegetables and one for green manures—in which plots are rotated yearly.

Intercropping

Intercropping refers to growing two or more crops together for greater productivity and more efficient use of resources. This practice is also referred to as undersowing or as a particular type of companion planting: the latter usually involves food crops intended for harvest, whereas undersowing most often indicates a leguminous green manure grown along with a food crop. White clover has been found to have the best prospects as an undersown cover crop that enriches the soil with nitrogen while not impeding the growth of most food crops. Many gardeners are familiar with the native North American tradition of companion planting corn, beans and squash—the beans growing up the corn and providing nitrogen, while the squash suppresses weeds. As I write, I have the personal example of my Dutch Capucijner soup peas (named for Capuchin friars) poking their pretty flowers between my knee-high garlic leaves. I sometimes plant winter cauliflower in the shade of corn or maturing fava beans. Russian winter kale is a very hardy and delicious winter green that often keeps my winter rye company, though I sow it much earlier for abundant winter picking.

Mulching

Mulching, like cover cropping, protects and enriches the soil and suppresses weeds admirably. Mulch materials are usually placed around growing plants or on ground where plants are soon to be. Thus mulch has more immediate benefits than green manures.

Benefits

Mulching prevents crusting of the soil surface and creates ideal seeding conditions at the interface of soil and mulch. It retains moisture and keeps the soil surface damp. This reduces the need to water as well as the amount of water required and allows the garden to be safely left for longer periods of time.

Mulching results in a light and fluffy porous soil that enhances root development and effective drainage. It keeps soil cooler in summer and warmer in fall and winter, prolonging the harvest of such crops as lettuce and peas and reducing the dangers of freezing and heaving. A thick layer of mulch prolongs root crop storage in the garden right where the vegetables grew. It supports weak or top-heavy plants and keeps sprawling vegetables mud-free and dry, preventing mildew, mold, rust and blight. Mulch is also effective in decreasing wind and water erosion from the sloping sides of raised beds.

The initial effort to mulch an area of the garden can seem very labor-intensive, but the effort saves a lot of time and energy (and sore backs) in the long run. It can eliminate most digging and all of the traditional "turning of the garden" in spring. This avoids disturbing the soil layers and preserves intricate earthworm tunnels. It also eliminates the need for most hoeing and weeding; weeds that do poke through after repeated mulching are weakly-rooted and easy to pull, or may be mulched over yet again.

Ruth Stout's Permanent Mulch System involves a year-round covering of the garden surface with continuously-added layers of organic material. In this system mulching becomes the main or on-going garden task and eliminates most of the weeding, hoeing and digging mentioned above. This gardener however, always stops short of such a total mulching scheme because of the pleasure and satisfaction I get from those very activities.

Disadvantages

Some hot weather crops may be slowed down somewhat by cooler soil under mulch. Avoid mulching if success with melons, squash, cukes and tomatoes is already chancy, or delay using mulch until the weather is hot. Plastic mulches, though not my choice for both aesthetic and environmental reasons, can help the earth absorb and retain heat, resulting in more vigorous growth.

Seedlings planted in very moist soil and mulched immediately can succumb to the soil-borne fungal disease called damping-off, which can eat through young stems in a matter of hours. Mulching on heavy water-logged soils can rot the crown and main roots of certain plants such as rhubarb. Again, mulching can be postponed until the soil is drier. Absorbent mulches already in place should be pulled back from the base of the plants to allow the soil to dry and ventilate.

Closely-planted rows, for instance in a bed of carrots, pose a special problem. This can be solved by sowing individual seeds and keeping the rows at least a hand's width apart. Pre-existing mulch, if it is not too thick, can be ridged up between the rows prior to planting. Thick mulch can be removed and used elsewhere. Sawdust or fine grass clippings are good mulches for closely-planted rows and can be brushed off the plants with the fingers to settle on the soil surface.

Perhaps the main objection to mulching is that it promotes and harbors slugs. I still haven't confirmed the validity of this objection. Until recently, I found hand picking at night or on rainy days to be the most effective method of slug control. Then, I decided to let the slugs have their way and experienced almost no slug damage of any consequence! In one of my worst slug thoroughfares, I applied a deep layer of straw, leaving it loose and bristly, and all my pea seedlings survived. (For non-believers, the list of recommended slug control methods includes snakes, toads, ducks, chickens, geese, traps, lures, barriers, beer, salt, sprays and wood ashes.)

Common Mulches

Beware when using hay as a mulch as it contains weed seeds—probably no problem in garden paths but definitely not the mulch to use in a bed of spring bulbs or in the onion patch. Straw, which is essentially the bare stalks left after the grain heads have been harvested, is one of the best all-round mulches, being lightweight, attractive and easy to handle.

Leaves are widely available, easy to handle and are excellent sources of humus when they break down into the soil.

Wood chips, wood shavings and shredded bark are best used for mulching garden paths. But don't take these from mills where they might be contaminated. They are usually applied several inches deep over a few layers of newspaper. They are not recommended as mulch for vegetables because they deplete soil nitrogen and take up to three years to decompose.

Sawdust, also when clean, is especially useful for spreading around small plants or along narrow footpaths. The best sawdust always comes from the bottom of the pile, so try for that.

Grass clippings are easy to obtain in summer and handy to spread in small places. Because of their nitrogen content they heat up readily, so avoid placing them against sensitive plant roots or stems.

When available and unpolluted, seaweed and lake weed make rich, soil-building mulches but follow the precautions given for grass clippings. I haven't found it necessary to wash salt from seaweed when using it in the garden.

Newspapers, when covered with a more visually pleasing mulch, are efficient in suppressing weeds but, except for those that have vegetable inks on non-bleached paper, will pollute your soil with lead and dioxins. Cardboard is unbleached and a more effective mulch material as well.

As already discussed, green manures can serve as living mulches that discourage weeds and enrich soil, but timely application is important.

Cover cropping and mulching are enjoying a vigorous renaissance as we become more conscious of how impoverished our gardens and food have become. Involving little financial investment, they act in a manner similar to composting, fostering earthworms, beneficial nematodes, bacteria and countless other organisms that enrich simple dirt and regenerate it into lush loam. They are basic and practical methods to create that organically rich soil that teems with life.

Part Two

Foods
For
Nutrition
And
Health

I n the early 1970s, *Diet for a Small Planet*, the best-selling book by Frances Moore Lappé, challenged many of the assumptions of my meat- and dairy-based diet, the prime one being the need for a large daily intake of protein of animal origin. Lappé asserted that we North Americans eat much more protein than our bodies can effectively utilize and that the quality of animal food we consume can be equalled simply by combining certain kinds of plant foods at each meal. Lappé's theories made sense to me: I believed I would be eating more efficiently and improving my health by eating lower off the food chain. However, although I did considerable experimentation with her recipes, something didn't quite work. Mostly, the meals I prepared were not very exciting. Certainly, they didn't reach the height of a juicy steak or even a Swiss cheese sandwich. Combining beans, grains, seeds and nuts at that time did little to change my culturally-conditioned belief that such foods were subsistence fare of less fortunate people.

I have now converted to plant foods as the mainstay of my diet and the reason I didn't do this twenty years ago is clearer to me now. Most of the foods advocated in *Diet for A Small Planet* that were available in health food stores were of poor quality. They were (and, for the most part, still are) so neglected by our food production and marketing system that what we could buy was often years old and/or not suitable for human consumption. For example, the promise of soybeans' wonderful nutritive qualities (including a 40 percent protein content) was never satisfyingly delivered by those obtainable in stores: after 24 hours soaking, many water changes and several hours cooking, they were still indigestible and insipid-tasting at best. Now I've returned to Lappé's recipes, knowing about and growing soybean cultivars that need only an hour's cooking after four hours soaking and that are both digestible and delectable.

As you will see in this section, there are many other high-protein plant foods that offer much more food quality than commonly believed. As these foods have assumed a more substantial part of my diet and as I've related more directly to people from other cultures, I've learned how unjustified my bias against these foods has been. The range and subtleties of taste and texture that I've discovered in beans and grains make my meals both satisfying and exciting. I am more and more appreciating that people worldwide have sustained themselves sumptuously on plant foods rather than having merely subsisted as is the common myth.

Twenty years after its first publication, *Diet for a Small Planet* continues to be a best-selling book. In later editions, Frances Moore Lappé has emphasized how our food production systems not only waste but also help destroy both renewable and non-renewable resources; as well, they deprive many people of their right to food. Her book is an inspiring source of ways and means to empower ourselves in the midst of such non-sustainable practices. To me, one of the simplest and most radical ways to do so is to grow our own food. Growing our own food reconnects us to the earth in ways not reached by any other social or political action. It is even more empowering, as I have been discovering for some years now, to garden with friends and neighbors. Community gardens, whether in rural or urban locations, enable people to join naturally together for mutual benefit.

A reconnection with the natural order of things is greatly needed at this time. The earth has grown inhospitable toward human presence as we have ceased to recognize the sacred character of habitat, as we have lost our sense of courtesy and gratitude towards the land and its inhabitants. Our quests for progress and development, for power and control over nature have brought us to a wasteworld instead of a wonderworld. Our sole standard for success in agriculture has been production: land and farmers have been asked only to produce and it has been assumed that competition and innovation would solve all problems. Agricultural practices for the past 50 years have given no importance to the preservation of the land, to its fertility and ecological health; they have ignored or defied our natural knowledge with the earth that sustains us.

People who use the land must know it well and must have the motivation and freedom to use it well. It is my belief that a renewal of such intimacy with the earth can be birthed by people reacquainting themselves with what gave birth to them eons ago. Food is of the earth and we also are of the earth. The meaning of such a simple truth eludes the corporate mind that is concerned only with economic return. Those of us who can convert grass into garden space, who can grow more life-sustaining foods, who can share space and energy resources with neighbors, who can live wisely and well off the bounty of our particular bioregion will serve as very powerful models of what is possible on a larger scale. Greening our gardens can catalyze a bold and viable new way of reinhabiting the Earth.

4

Beans, Beans, Glorious Food!

The myriad colors, shapes and sizes of dry beans are as thrilling to the gardener as sun-bright, surf-washed pebbles are to the veteran beachcomber. Winking out winter-long through the polished sides of clear glass jars, they may also lure the modern-day alchemist in search of a perfect meal.

Dried beans, to my mind, are the most undervalued of garden vegetables. I say this after fifteen years of growing my own food, four years of managing a seed company, and a persistent compulsion to dive right into the gardening articles whenever horticultural journals arrive.

In early May '90 I sowed over 120 varieties of dried beans at Mansell Farm on Salt Spring Island, B.C. Situated in the Gulf of Georgia between Vancouver and Victoria at 49°N. and 123°W., Salt Spring doesn't get the concentrated summer heat familiar to most continental growers. Summer days rarely go above 80°F (27°C). Annual rainfall is about 39 inches (100 cm), most of which falls between October and April. By the first week in September I had harvested all but a dozen of those varieties and had used no irrigation. So, unless you're at a latitude or an elevation where there are less than 100 frost free days, don't let concerns about getting dried beans to mature thwart your desire to grow them.

Bean Varieties

I've made it my business to popularize dried beans because my family and I have become increasingly impressed by their versatility and food value as well as their easy culture and storage. For families interested in becoming protein self-sufficient, growing dried beans is an excellent place to start. Many gardeners believe beans are not worth their growing space because of low yields and cheap availability. But I have found dozens of high-yielding, short season and great-tasting dried beans that are not offered by stores or seed companies. As with almost all home grown food, your own dried beans will taste better than store-bought varieties. Not only are garden-grown beans more easily digested, they also demand you highlight rather than bury their taste under condiments and spices. In time, you may become so intimate with the nuance and bounty of bean flavors that you'll reach for Montezuma Reds, Santa Maria Pinquitos or Ireland Creek Annies with as much authority as you now do for Cheddar, Swiss or Camembert!

Classification

Beans are divided into snap, shell and dry varieties depending on their stage of development at harvest. (Soybeans and garbanzos—or chickpeas—are botanically different.) Snap or string beans, also called green or yellow beans, are picked fresh from early summer on, when their seeds are still undeveloped or very small. The gardener wants tender pods, not chewy beans. Shell beans, such as limas or horticultural beans, are harvested when the beans are fully formed but not dried out. Dry beans are harvested when they rattle in the pods.

There is some overlapping of the types: certain snap beans and horticultural beans can be left to mature into quite good dry beans, and some dry beans are quite tasty at the green shell stage, as are soybeans. I discovered only recently that most dry beans make fine green beans as well and can be harvested for as long a period as normal snap beans. Dry beans may have strings, which should be removed if the pods will be eaten. Snap off the head and tail of the bean, and the string will come along too.

Bush and Pole Beans

You'll want to consider whether to choose a bush or a pole variety of dry bean. Pole beans grow six-feet to eight- feet (2-2 1/2 m) tall by twining around sticks, strings or wires: strong supports, such as trellises or tepees are best in place before or soon after the seeds are sown. Bush types are self-supporting and grow only to two or three feet (0.6-0.9 m). As far as flavor is concerned, I personally find that pole dry beans don't surpass bush dry beans, though some are as good. Because they are less work, I grow mostly the bush varieties.

Maturation

The number of days to maturity is another important factor when choosing varieties. Jacob's Cattle, Soldier and Yellow Eye are listed at about 90 days in most catalogues and are generally considered the earliest beans. The first beans to dry in my garden (at just under 100 days), however, are Squaw Yellow, Limelight and Buckskin. Most of the rest—including the first three mentioned as well as pinto, navy, chili, black, soy, garbanzo, Swedish and Dutch beans—take about 110 days in this maritime climate. My Squaw Yellow are ready to pick in mid-August from an early-May planting. I grow a few later-maturing beans, such as Gnuttle Amish and Santa Maria Pinquito, because their superior taste and texture make it worth chancing the weather. I have had some success with lima beans and adzuki beans but usually don't harvest these as dry beans until early October.

Yield

Yield is also significant when choosing varieties and some very popular beans may not provide an abundant harvest. For example, a 50-foot (15-m) row of Jacob's Cattle beans usually provides half the four or five pounds (1.8-2.3 kg) of dry beans I'd harvest from another variety. However yield is determined by many factors: many of my far-flung seed customers to whom I have sent Jacob's Cattle beans report harvests of over five pounds per same length row. I have occasionally had early and abundant yields from supermarket dry beans, especially navy and kidney. Aesthetic appeal is another consideration: many dry beans are so pretty that a child's delight in shelling them might overshadow the importance of yield.

If you save and plant seed from your earliest and highest-yielding plants, you'll have your own locally-adapted strain in a few years. Once you have a type you like that does well for you, you need never purchase seed again.

Growing Dry Beans

There is an important consideration to note when choosing a planting site for dry beans. Green and shell beans are usually harvested when the summer sun is still high. Because dry beans take about six weeks longer to reach full maturity and because you want to harvest their pods at maximum dryness, plant them where they will continue to receive sun on August and September afternoons.

Requirements

Beans are very easy to grow. Though they are at their best in warm, moderately rich soil, they do well in a wide range of soils, even without fertilizer. In especially acidic soil (below a pH of 6.0) the addition of bonemeal, wood ashes, dolomite lime or compost will, by their alkaline nature, moderate the acidity. In a very sandy soil that leeches nutrients easily, nitrogen should be added, but bear in mind that too much will promote excessive leaf growth, plus delay and reduce pod production.

Nitrogen is important for good bean growth, but, because they're legumes, beans can fix their own nitrogen from the air through the action of *Rhizobium* bacteria that live in nodules on their roots. Thus beans are an excellent crop for enriching your soil. In a new garden however, it's worth coating your bean seed with an inoculant containing the proper type of *Rhizobium*, carried at most garden shops, to ensure their presence. Once these bacteria are in the soil, they multiply rapidly and persist indefinitely. Soybeans have a bacteria inoculant specific to them, as do other legumes. Be sure to check the expiration date on *Rhizobium* obtained from garden centres to ensure the bacteria are still active.

Planting

Most catalogues and gardening books suggest planting beans just after the last estimated spring frost date. On the coast here, where the last frost occurs in March or even February, but the soil does not warm quickly, I wait until at least early May to ensure good, even germination. Beans are a warm-weather crop and there is little to be gained by having them shiver through their early growth. On a small scale, planting beans in raised beds saves a lot of space and work. Raised beds also heat up more quickly in spring to allow an earlier sowing. Soaking beans beforehand is not usually worth it when they are going into cold soil anyway. Because presoaking often results in cracked seed and more difficult sowing, I would recommend it only for late-season starts.

Planting my dry beans in rows a foot and a half (45 cm) apart allows me to do most of my weeding by rototilling between the rows until the bean plants fill the open areas and block out weeds. I sow the seed a little over an inch (3 cm) deep, using a hand row seeder (an efficient and inexpensive tool for large gardens), and later thin the seedlings to a few inches apart to allow for adequate air circulation around the plants.

Maintenance

Bean diseases seldom ruin a backyard harvest. During the dozen years I've been growing beans on Salt Spring Island, I've seen no bean diseases and only a few aphids and bean beetles. It is worth taking precautions, however. Don't risk spreading rusts, mildews or blights by working among wet plants. Remove or turn under bean debris when the plants are finished. Gardening guides recommend rotating the location of the bean crop from year to year for disease and pest management. However, I broke that rule in 1989 and had my one of my best harvests ever! I credit the abundance of nitrogen-fixing bacteria still in the soil from the previous crop, but I didn't press my luck by growing beans three years in the same spot.

Dry beans aren't "dry" until three to four months after planting, so until then, the main tasks are watering, weeding or mulching, and watching for insects or disease. Most bush beans help keep the soil from drying out by their spreading habit. Mulch, if available, can greatly reduce the need to water and weed. The most crucial time to ensure adequate soil moisture is during pod and seed formation; fewer and smaller beans will result if the plants stay thirsty at this time. Beans are fairly drought tolerant. In fact, I had bumper harvests in both 1989 and 1990 without any mulching or watering.

Harvesting

With short-season varieties, anyone blessed with a hot, sunny site can have a crop that dries to perfection in the garden. The leaves fall off the plants and the pods turn brown. On hot days, the pods start spilling their beans; pick them before too many have fallen. To ensure that the pods are thoroughly dry, bring them indoors to a warm, dry place with good air circulation. Many varieties ripen over a week or two, and it's best to go through the patch every few days to pick the driest.

If you're experimenting with different varieties, you'll find that many longer-season ones do not reach the drying stage until September or October, when rain and fog are common. If the weather is dismal, pull the entire plants and hang them upside down in a well-ventilated greenhouse, shed, barn, attic or basement. Do this also if frost threatens, as bean plants are killed by only a few degrees of frost. As long as the crop is close to maturity, the seeds will continue to ripen in the pods even after they've been removed from the plant. Even relatively immature beans may ripen this way. If the pods are damp when picked, but the weather is clear, spread them on tarps in a sunny place to prevent the growth of mold. If they are already dry, store the pods indoors and stir them occasionally until the beans reach their full color.

Threshing

I place the dry pods on waist-high tables in a greenhouse and at the end of one or two hot days, I thresh them by hand in a matter of minutes. The method is actually closer to kneading than threshing; as I work through the dry pods with my fingers, the shelled beans quickly go to the bottom and the split pods stay on top. An alternate and quite enjoyable method of shelling the pods is to place them in a box, chest or trough and to then walk/shuffle over them. It is most important in this case that the beans be totally dry or they will be crushed. Bean-by-bean shelling with friends can be a fine social event, especially when later completed by a festive bean bake.

Until a few years ago I cleaned threshed beans by putting them in a large bowl outdoors and then blowing the chaff away with a hair dryer. All the while, I'd screen out any debris or weed seeds and discard any moldy or discolored beans by hand. Then I discovered the air compressor, previously reserved for filling truck and tractor tires. The right nozzle attachment and degree of pressure directed at my bucket of beans gets the job done in a few minutes.

Storing

When beans are sufficiently dry, a thumbnail cannot dent them. Some catalogues recommend putting beans in the freezer for a few days to kill any bean weevils that could damage the crop in storage, but I have yet to find any of the small holes in beans that are the telltale signs of weevils. If you decide to follow the freezing procedure, give the beans a little extra drying after removing them, as beans placed in the freezer collect some moisture. Store dried beans in labelled jars on a cool, dry shelf.

Beans as Food

With the exception of soybeans, the beans I've mentioned are indigenous to the Western Hemisphere. They were introduced to Europe in the 16th and 17th centuries, later to return, somewhat disguised, to North America. Most of the world's cuisines have wonderful bean-based dishes, but in Central and South America it's been beans for 7,000 years!

Cooked dry beans are delicious in a wide variety of main and side dishes. They are a nourishing, versatile staple, each kind with its own flavor and texture. Unfortunately, most cookbooks are short on information about preparing them. Here are some tips, as well as a few recipes to get you started.

Cooking

The flatulence factor in beans is a major concern for many people. One tested method for reducing gas caused by beans is to change the soaking water two or three times, replenishing the pot with fresh water each time. Rinsing beans after they've been soaked also removes gas-promoting substances. (The loss of B vitamins and protein by not cooking beans in their soaking water is only one to three percent.) Cooking beans thoroughly is also important: uncooked starch is obviously harder to digest. Do not add baking soda as some books suggest: it reduces flavor and nutrition by making the water too alkaline, it can toughen the beans, and it doesn't lessen the offending substances. Also, do not add salt to the soaking or cooking water: it reacts with the seed coat and prevents absorption of liquids. Beyond these precautions, the best way to avoid flatulence is to cook home-grown beans! I'm not really sure why this is so, though I've convinced myself and others of it with many meals. My guess is that chemical changes transpire as beans age, making them less digestible when cooked.

Homegrown beans do not need as much soaking or cooking as purchased beans do. The usual recommendation of an overnight soaking is mostly for convenience, because some beans will have been lying around for years. Relatively fresh beans absorb all the water they can in four hours. Use three or four times as much water as beans. If you don't have time for a long soak, place washed and sorted beans in a large pot, cover them with three or four times their volume of fresh water, heat and hold them at a boil for two minutes. Then remove the pot from the heat, and leave it covered for an hour. Rinse the beans, and they will be ready to cook. The final product will not be as mellow as it should be, because beans have a better texture if they absorb water slowly; nevertheless, the loss of nutrients from the quick-soaking method is negligible.

After four hours of soaking, most homegrown beans need 50 minutes of cooking, but black soybeans need about 90 minutes, and some navy beans take as long as two hours. To cook pre-soaked beans in a pot, cover them with fresh cold water, bring to a boil, reduce heat, partially cover the pot to prevent foaming and simmer for the indicated length of time. When using a pressure cooker, make sure the pot is no more than half full, and cook at 15 pounds (7 kg) pressure for 15 to 25 minutes. Some beans, especially soybeans, have a tendency to bubble up through the pressure valve during cooking. To prevent this, add a tablespoonful (15 mL) of vegetable oil per cup (250 mL) of beans before cooking. Oil also helps reduce foam when using a conventional saucepan.

Texture

The texture of cooked beans can greatly enhance their appeal, so it's important to know how long to cook them. Cooking them for just under an hour leaves most of the beans I grow with a little chewiness to complement their taste. Pressure-cooked beans inevitably have a soft-textured inside and a tender skin. Do not cook beans in a sauce in an effort to soften and flavor them at the same time: many ingredients tend to halt the tenderizing process. But if you add cooked beans to a sauce, their texture will not change.

Recipes

The following recipes are three of my family's favorites. We enjoy discovering what best enhances each unique bean flavor.

Black Soy Express

The hearty taste of black soybeans is complemented rather than camouflaged by the ingredients in this simple recipe. (Serves 4)

1 cup	dry black soybeans	250 mL
1 Tbsp	cooking oil	15 mL
1 tsp	ginger, freshly grated	5 mL
1/2 tsp	cumin	2.5 mL
2	garlic cloves, chopped fine	
3	leeks, chopped	
1 Tbsp	miso	15 mL
1 tsp	molasses	5 mL
1/4 cup	parsley (preferably Italian), chopped	50 mL

Soak the soybeans overnight or for a minimum of 4 hours. Cover beans with at least twice the volume of fresh, cold water, and add oil. Heat to boiling and simmer for 1 1/2 hours.

In a skillet over medium heat, cook the ginger, cumin and garlic for several minutes. Add leeks and sauté until golden.

Dilute the miso in a small amount of warm water and combine with molasses.

Combine everything with the drained soybeans and cook on stovetop for 20 minutes. Shortly before serving, stir in parsley.

Serve with rice.

BLACK BEAN THANKSGIVING

This dish is especially festive if the main ingredients are fresh from the garden. (Serves 6-8)

1 cup	dried Black Turtle Soup beans	250 mL
4 Tbsp	cooking oil	60 mL
4	medium onions, coarsely chopped	
2 Tbsp	garlic, chopped	30 mL
6 cups	Italian plum tomatoes, chopped	1500 mL
1	medium-sized winter squash, cooked	
1 Tbsp	green/red chili or jalapeño peppers, finely chopped	15 mL
2 Tbsp	orange rind, chopped	30 mL
1/2 cup	raisins	125 mL
1/2 tsp	cinnamon	2.5 mL
1/2 tsp	allspice	2.5 mL
1/2 tsp	nutmeg	2.5 mL
1/4 tsp	ground cloves	1.25 mL
2	large tart apples, peeled, cored and cubed	
	Salt and freshly ground pepper to taste	

Soak the beans for 4 hours. Heat to boiling in a large pot and simmer for 1 hour.

Sauté onions and garlic in oil in a large skillet until golden. Stir in tomatoes, squash, peppers, orange pieces, raisins and spices and simmer uncovered for 20-30 minutes.

Stir in drained beans and apples. Simmer for 10 minutes.

Serve with oven-roasted potatoes.

Three Bean Salad

This variation of a traditional salad is greatly enhanced by the colors, textures and freshness inherent in home-grown beans. It can include as many varieties as you like. Red and white kidney beans with black garbanzos or black soybeans make an appealing combination. (Serves 4-6)

1 1/2 cups	dry beans	375 mL
1/2 cup	leeks, shallots or chives, minced	125 mL
6 Tbsp	olive oil	90 mL
2 Tbsp	fresh lemon juice	30 mL
2 Tbsp	dill or basil, chopped	30 mL
1/2 tsp	sea salt (to taste)	2.5 mL
1/2 tsp	tamari	2.5 mL
	Pinch of cayenne pepper	

Soak beans in separate pots for a minimum of 4 hours. Heat to boiling and simmer until desired texture is reached. Drain and chill.

Thoroughly mix all ingredients in a bowl.

Make appealing individual servings by putting half a cup or more of the mixture on to Romaine or other leaf lettuce. Garnish with a lemon wedge, a sprig of parsley, fresh dill, chervil or chive flowers.

Beans for the Planet

My family has substituted beans for most meat and dairy foods for several years now. Our bodies feel lighter, healthier and more responsive for the switch. It's also good to know that we are not contributing to an industry that is anything but friendly to the environment or to the animals it processes. To me, one of the obvious ways we can begin to clean up our polluted earth is to grow high-protein crops that constitute good human food and do well in North America. It takes 16 pounds of feed and 2500 gallons of water to produce one pound of beef. Between

22 and 44 times less fossil fuel is required to produce beans and grains rather than meat. It seems folly to grow beans to prepare millions of animals for slaughter when we could be eating them ourselves for better health and nutrition. Compared to other protein sources and vegetables, dry beans don't have to be refrigerated, frozen, canned or packaged in plastic.

Beans for Health

If you want to take greater responsibility for your own health, you might consider beans for many reasons. Only recently has the medical profession begun to give importance to the glaring fact that degenerative diseases are almost unheard of where diets include large quantities of beans and other fibre foods. As cultures replace beans and other complex carbohydrates with foods loaded with fats and cholesterol, there is a corresponding increase in cardiovascular diseases, intestinal ailments, cancers of the digestive system, appendicitis, gallstones, diverticulosis, hiatus hernia, hemorrhoids and diabetes. Has this not happened in our own culture?

Beans have many factors in their favor. They are one of the five least allergenic foods. They are high in protein and are well-endowed with thiamine, niacin, B-6 and folic acid as well as calcium, iron, phosphorous and potassium. The fibre in beans helps keep the digestive system clean and promotes regularity.

Beans are a boon to diabetics, hypoglycemics and those on weight-loss diets. For one, they retain water in the digestive tract, which promotes a feeling of fullness and delays the return of hunger. In addition, only two to six percent of the calories in beans are derived from fat, in contrast to 75 to 85 percent for meat and cheese. The only exception is soybeans, which have 34 percent fat calories. As with all beans though, the fat is polyunsaturated and less harmful than the fat in animal products. Beans are cholesterol-free, and recent research shows that they even contain a chemical that fights the deposit of fat globules in veins and arteries. Not only do they control blood cholesterol, they also control glucose. Unlike other carbohydrate foods, such as bread, cereals, potatoes and pasta, beans don't trigger a rise in blood sugar or require that the pancreas pour out extra insulin to readjust the glucose level in the blood.

From garden to table, beans are simple foods that come just as nature made them. Like Jack of beanstalk fame, I have been seduced by the richness generated from my first planting of a handful of beans. I'm only just discovering the carnival of delights they offer!

5

Protein Foods Of South America

In the past few years I have become increasingly delighted and enthusiastic about two very old, high-protein plants that hail from South America, and are relatively new to us. Both quinoa (keen' wah) and amaranth have a 5000-year track record and early indicators show they hold great promise and potential for self-sustaining gardens in the northern hemisphere too. They grow as easily as their weedy relatives and the quality of food they offer far surpasses that of our common grains. Traditional hand-harvesting methods can obtain bounteous harvests from these sacred crops of the Incas and Aztecs.

Two Remarkable Plants

Quinoa and amaranth are treated as grains although they have broad leaves, unlike the true grains and corn, which are grasses. Their leaves are among the most nutritious of vegetable greens, but it is their fruit that is meant when these plants are referred to as "crops." And that fruit or grain is quite unique. The protein content of these two foods has an essential amino acid balance close to the ideal. In fact, they both come closer to meeting the ideal protein requirements of the human body than either cow's milk or soybeans. They are high in the amino acid lysine, which is lacking in most cereals such as wheat, sorghum, corn and barley. Relatively small amounts of these grains mixed with amaranth or quinoa in baked goods provides complete protein.

Both quinoa and amaranth are very adaptable, disease-free and drought-tolerant plants. They thrive in rich soil—as long as it is well drained—but both will, once established, produce abundant harvests under quite dry conditions.

Quinoa has been introduced to North America in the past decade, mainly through the efforts of the Quinoa Corporation of Boulder, Colorado. Amaranth has been popularized by *Organic Gardening Magazine*—many of whose readers and researchers have been testing and selecting varieties for fifteen years and continue to do so.

The wild relatives of both amaranth and quinoa have long been familiar to North American gardeners and are often called by the same name of pigweed. The pigweed that is related to quinoa is also called lamb's-quarters (*Chenopodium album*), while the ancestor of amaranth is known as red-rooted pigweed or wild amaranth (*Amaranthus retroflexus*). Both pigweeds have the amazing ability to flower and go to seed at any stage of their growth and both will cross with their cultivated progeny. The grower who wants pure strains of either quinoa or amaranth must therefore pay close attention to weeds.

Most cultivars of amaranth and quinoa grow four- to six-feet (1.2 to 1.8 m) high and, when in flower, are majestic plants whose presence emits a special radiance in any garden. Quinoa's unique flower hues are most striking at a close distance around dawn or dusk, while amaranth's flamboyant bronze and burgundy tones are dazzling in bright sunshine. Smaller ornamental amaranths such as Love-lies-bleeding and

Prince's-feather have been listed in garden catalogues for hundreds of years.

Quinoa

I first heard about quinoa in 1985 from the Abundant Life Seed Foundation in Port Townsend, Washington. I was intrigued by its story. Quinoa is an annual plant of the goosefoot family, closely resembling its relative, lamb's-quarters, until it spurts up to shoulder height and develops its large seedhead loaded with millet-like seeds. It has been commonly grown at high altitudes throughout the Andes of South America for at least 5000 years. About ten million descendants of the Inca Empire, from southern Chile and Argentina through Bolivia, Peru, and Ecuador still use quinoa as an important component of their daily diet.

Quinoa contains 16 percent protein, E and B vitamins, calcium, iron and phosphorous. It is easy to digest, has a wonderful flavor, and cooks up whole, like rice, in 15 minutes. It is also an extremely hardy plant that thrives in places where few other plants survive. Because it does so well at high elevations, most North American quinoa research has been done in the Rocky Mountains of Colorado. However, Abundant Life Seed Foundation has been testing quinoa varieties in low-elevation, maritime conditions, since 1979.

I sowed my first packets of quinoa seed in early May of 1986. I broadcast four different varieties in small patches, gently raking the ground so that the tiny seed would be just under the soil surface. It wasn't until a month later that I realized that some of the succulent lamb's-quarters, or pigweed, that I'd been weeding and munching were likely baby quinoa plants. I stopped weeding the patches entirely then and waited until I could identify the quinoa for certain. By late August, the quinoa were clearly identifiable by their larger and more colorful seedheads. They were only three- to four-feet (about a metre) high when I harvested them in late September. I assumed they had been stunted by weed competition and put away my small yield to be planted in distinguishable rows the following year.

My 1987 crop did much better when planted in rows, but although weeding was much less confusing, I spent many hours thinning. Every seed must have germinated and even after the third thinning I wasn't yet at the eight-inch (20-cm) interval recommended by Abundant Life. I resolved to mix some sand or radish seed with the quinoa seed when sowing the following year. I had staggered plantings and found that there wasn't any advantage to planting before early May in the cool valley bottom conditions of the Salt Spring Centre where I was gardening. When the plants were drying down and losing their leaves in mid-September, I pulled some of them and hung them to dry in the greenhouse. The plants outside dried equally well, thanks to Salt Spring's typically fine fall weather, and threshed well too. My technique for threshing was to bend the seedheads over into a bucket and rub them between the palms of my hands. The chaff was easy to blow away with the help of a hair dryer.

Finally, after two years, I had enough quinoa to try eating some. However, I knew the small seeds were covered with a bitter substance called *saponin*, which birds and deer won't touch. Because of this coating, quinoa requires thorough washing before cooking. I followed Abundant Life's suggestion of putting the grain in a blender with cool water at lowest speed and changing the water until it was no longer soapy. It took about six water changes to achieve the desired, non-frothy result. I cooked the quinoa following the basic recipe and was impressed and delighted: it was delicious and had a very pleasing texture. Everyone I tested it on agreed, and most people categorically responded: "This tastes great!"

In the spring of 1988, I also sowed quinoa at Mansell Farm, which is warmer and drier than the Salt Spring Centre. By this time I had divided my quinoa into two types. Because I could detect little difference between three of the varieties, I had combined them, and was calling them "multi-hued" quinoa; the other variety had only yellowish seedheads and was named "Dave #407" in honor of plant explorer Dave Cusack, who was instrumental in introducing quinoa to North American agriculture.

During the first week of May I planted my quinoa with a row seeder in 125-foot (40-m) rows at the Salt Spring Centre and in 300-foot (90-m) rows at Mansell Farm. The seedlings were visible in a week. I deliberately planted the rows to just accommodate an 18-inch (45-cm) rototiller between them, which worked perfectly for weed control. I rototilled in early and late June and did some occasional weeding and thinning between the plants. The quinoa at Mansell Farm was knee-high by the end of June and was starting to flower early in July. The quinoa at the cooler, Salt Spring Centre site, flowered a few weeks later. Both plantings grew robustly with no irrigation and only a few rainy days all summer. The Dave quinoa averaged four feet (1.2 m), and the multi-hued, six feet (1.8 m).

I had a joyous surprise from the multi-hued quinoa because I had never really noticed how magnificent their flower heads were. The many hours I spent weeding out the bindweed twisting around their stalks were probably the highlight of my gardening year. The flowers have unique flower tones of mauve, purple, red, orange, green and yellow. They are not flamboyant but have a subtle brilliance: they need to be absorbed for a while, especially in morning or evening light, to be fully appreciated. I managed to drop my workaholic self and bathe in the glory of those long quinoa rows. Ironically, weeding the bindweed had been totally unnecessary: just the right screen turned up later and I could sift the quinoa quickly to discard the larger bindweed seeds.

More quinoa surprises were in store for me. I started harvesting at Mansell Farm early in September when practically all the leaves had fallen from the plants. I used my old technique of rubbing the tops between my palms into buckets. The seedheads were so dry that I soon discovered the much quicker method of stripping the stalk with my thumb and fingers. I also discovered that the proper pressure valve on the air compressor mentioned in the bean chapter speeded the winnowing process to a matter of minutes. Harvesting bliss! In the midst of my jubilation, however, there was a heavy rain halfway through the harvesting. The next day I was presented with the disappointing sight of multi-hued quinoa sprouting right on their stalks. The Dave quinoa weren't sprouting but I had immediate trepidations as to their viability. To my chagrin I soon found that none of the Dave quinoa had more than 20 to 30 percent viability.

Although the 1988 growing season was over, my quinoa discoveries were only beginning. I was at our Farmer's Market in Ganges one late September morning, selling garlic as well as some quinoa I had packaged for Salt Spring Seeds—something I felt was a unique commodity in

Canada at that point. I was amazed when a farmer visiting from Ontario noticed my quinoa packets and told me he had not long before harvested a successful few acres of quinoa in North Bay and also that he knew of another Ontario farmer who had harvested five acres from an early June planting. Don's main concern was how to remove the bitter saponin covering the seed. All I could tell him was that I knew the technology existed because cleaned quinoa was available in health food stores in Vancouver, Victoria, and indeed in two stores not far from where we were standing. The two U.S. companies marketing quinoa were the Quinoa Corporation and Eden Foods. The Quinoa Corporation didn't elaborate on how it cleaned its Colorado quinoa; Eden Foods mechanically desaponized its Ecuadorian quinoa by a rubbing process similar to polishing rice. I told Don I had just discovered the best way yet of washing small amounts of quinoa prior to cooking: by tying the desired amount in a stocking, a loose weave muslin bag, or a pillow case and running it through the cold water cycles of an automatic washing machine.

My conversation with Don led me to write the Manitoba, Saskatchewan, and Alberta departments of agriculture to see if anyone had heard of quinoa or of anyone growing it. Further surprises: crop specialists wrote back saying that quinoa had been successfully grown in the last year in each of the prairie provinces, and that it was easily harvested using traditional combining methods. Although some farmers processed the quinoa on their own farms and could distribute it through health food markets, other farmers had no way of cleaning off the saponin and found few available commercial markets. Weeds were a problem in some fields as no herbicides or pesticides were registered for use on quinoa in Canada. The crop specialists sent me lots of information. One particularly useful tidbit was that warm quinoa seeds planted in warm soil might not germinate. I immediately put my heretofore 20 to 30 percent viable Dave quinoa back into sprouting jars and soaked them in cool water in my garage. In 24 hours I had over 90 percent germination!

I also received interesting statistics on yields. From my 1988 plantings which yielded about two pounds (1 kg) per 50-foot (15-m) row, I estimated that I could realistically expect to harvest about 1200 pounds (500 kg) per acre on Salt Spring Island. This was confirmed by the yields of some of the prairie farmers although yields of up to 2000 pounds (over 900 kg) per acre are considered possible given increased expertise and better-adapted varieties.

For the home gardener however, harvests might be much more impressive on rich soils. While I was getting about an ounce (28 gm) of seed per plant, my friend Biz was getting over six ounces (169 gm) per plant grown in her best compost. Most of her stalks were eight- to nine-feet (2.4- to 2.7-m) high with massive seedheads, two of which were thrilling sights at Salt Spring's Fall Fair. Biz' results clearly indicated to me the possibility of huge harvests if we babied quinoa the way we usually do corn or lettuce or broccoli. Biz also found that she could get away with less or no rinsing by mixing quinoa with other grains or pulses, where the saponin will be hardly noticeable.

Quinoa had a few more surprises for me in 1989. Despite all the quinoa that had sprouted during the 1988 harvest rain, I discovered the following spring thousands of self-sown baby quinoa plants in that old multi-hued quinoa patch. It would have been interesting to see if I could establish a "perennial" quinoa area but as there were already other plans for that ground, that's still a future project. 1989 was also the year I first saw the aborted seedheads I had heard about from a few gardeners to whom I had supplied seed. These plants' flowers shrivelled up for no apparent reason, even though they'd been looking as healthy as the rest of the crop, which went on to yield an abundant harvest. Because this occurred during a spell of very high temperatures, this could reflect quinoa's current non-adaptability to very hot weather at seed formation time. On the other hand, I will be looking to discover if some insect has found my quinoa to its liking.

In 1990, Abundant Life Seed Foundation offered for the first time a variety of quinoa that is essentially saponin-free and can be eaten just as it comes from the harvest without excess washing. It is late maturing and comparatively low in yield. I have started to grow this variety and intend to do some selecting from it for earliness and higher yield.

Cultural Considerations

Quinoa grows best where maximum temperatures do not exceed 90°F (32°C) and nighttime temperatures are cool. For most southern Canadian and northern U.S. sites, the best time to plant quinoa is late April to late May. When soil temperatures are around 60°F (15°C) seedlings emerge within three to four days. However, when warm quinoa seeds are planted in soil with night-time temperature much above that, quinoa, like spinach, may not germinate. In this instance, it's best to refrigerate seeds before planting.

As mentioned earlier, quinoa resembles lamb's-quarters, especially in the early stages of growth, so it is best to sow seed in rows to make weeding less confusing. Since quinoa seed is small (0.1 inch or 2-3 mm in diameter), you can avoid considerable thinning by mixing it with sand or radish seed before sowing, as is sometimes done with carrots. Planting can be done by hand or with a row seeder. Seeds should be planted about a quarter- to a half-inch (1-cm) deep. Optimum spacing after a month or so will be two to four plants per foot (30 cm) of row, although in very fertile soil a foot between plants is more advisable. Rows can be one and a half to two feet (45-60 cm) apart, or wide enough to accommodate a rototiller between the rows without damaging the plants. One gram of seed will sow 50 feet (15 m) of row. An acre requires about one pound (0.5 kg) of seed.

Soil moisture is probably sufficient until late May to germinate the seed. Excessive water will kill quinoa plants. Given good soil moisture, don't water until the plants reach the two- or three-leaf stage. Quinoa appears slow growing at first but is extremely drought tolerant and does well on a total of 10 to 15 inches (25 to 40 cm) of water.

Quinoa is responsive to nitrogen and phosphorous. Plants grown in good garden soil will be four feet to six feet (120- to 180 cm) tall, while those grown in compost may reach over eight feet (2.5 m).

Harvesting

Most quinoa varieties resist light frosts especially if the soil is dry. As long as maturing seed is past the green stage, frost will cause little damage and harvesting can be done a day or two later. Extreme hot weather and warm nights inhibit fruit set. It is important to watch the weather when quinoa is ready to be harvested: if rained on, the dry seed will germinate. If the heads are not completely dry, harvest them when you can barely indent the seeds with your thumbnail. They should then be thoroughly dried before storage.

Cooking Tips

My wife, Alison, and I have tried some of the recipes which came with the original seed packets from Abundant Life (published by the Quinoa Corporation) and we've made up some of our own. Quinoa's simple distinctive taste gives it great versatility for cooking purposes and it can be substituted for almost any grain in almost any recipe. Because it is not a true cereal grain, it can be eaten by people who suffer from cereal grain allergies.

The basic quinoa recipe can be written in a sentence: Bring two cups of water and one cup of rinsed quinoa to a boil, reduce to a simmer, cover, and cook until all water is absorbed, about 12 to 15 minutes. Cooked quinoa expands almost five times its dry volume and turns transparent. The bands around the periphery of the disk-shaped seeds partially separate but retain their curved shape, making quinoa look like it is sprinkled with little spirals or crescent moons. These little bands offer just enough tooth resistance to give quinoa a texture similar to that of wild rice. One of our favorite preparations is very simple: it makes a great hash when sautéed with cooked squash and a little onion.

We have yet to try quinoa flour. Though lacking gluten, it can undoubtedly enhance the taste and nutritional quality of countless dishes.

Quinoa greens make tasty salad material and have a high vitamin and mineral content similar to that of lamb's-quarters. We've juiced carrots with a small amount of quinoa leaves—a most invigorating drink.

Recipes

Quinoa Tabouli

Tabouli, a mid-eastern salad normally made with bulgur wheat, makes light and refreshing, warm weather fare. Try it with quinoa for a delightful new taste. (Serves 4)

QUINOA TABOULI *cont'd.*

2 cups	quinoa, cooked	500 mL
1 cup	parsley, chopped	250 mL
1/2 cup	scallions, chopped	125 mL
2 tbsp	fresh mint	25 mL
1 tsp	basil	5 mL
1/2 cup	lemon juice	125 mL
1/4 cup	olive oil	75 mL
2	garlic cloves, pressed	
1/4 cup	olives, sliced	75 mL
	lettuce leaves, whole	

Place all ingredients except lettuce and olives in a mixing bowl and toss together lightly. Chill for an hour or more to allow flavors to blend.

Wash and dry lettuce leaves and use them to line a salad bowl. Add tabouli and garnish with olives.

QUINOA PUDDING

This quick and wholesome dessert is also elegant and tasty. (Serves 4)

2 cups	quinoa, cooked	500 mL
1 cup	apple juice	250 mL
1/2 cup	raisins	125 mL
1/2 cup	almonds, chopped	125 mL
1 1/2 tsp	vanilla	8 mL
	juice of 1/2 lemon	
	grated rind of one lemon	
	dash of cinnamon	

Combine ingredients in a large sauce pan, cover and bring to a boil. Reduce heat and simmer for 15 minutes.

Pour pudding into individual dessert bowls. Top with a few grapes or strawberries.

Serve chilled.

Amaranth

Amaranth was the sacred food as well as the main grain crop of the Aztecs. The Spanish Conquistadores, disturbed by its use in Aztec religious ceremonies, forbade them to grow amaranth on pain of having their hands cut off, but its cultivation continued secretly. Unlike quinoa, amaranth has not been confined to South America. It was a symbol of immortality for the ancient Greeks and they praised its exceptional healing qualities. The cultures of India, China and Japan contain many legends and sacred rituals surrounding amaranth and its ability to bring long life and health.

Cultural Considerations

Amaranth is a warm season crop that requires full sun. Best germination occurs when soil temperatures range from 65 to 75°F (18-24°C). Optimum soil is a well-drained loam but amaranths will do well in all but poorly aerated clay soils. Their small seeds require a finely prepared surface and adequate moisture until the first set of true leaves appear. Seeds should be sown no more than one-quarter inch (6-mm) deep in rows 18 inches (45 cm) apart and plants should eventually be thinned 10 to 18 inches (25-45 cm) apart. Transplanting does not work very well with amaranth seedlings.

Amaranth is a low-maintenance crop but weeds, especially at the beginning, should be discouraged by cultivation or mulching. Growth is slow during the first few weeks but as the plants reach about one foot (30 cm) in height, they start to grow very rapidly, the canopy closes in and weeds are shaded out. Amaranth likes phosphorous and nitrogen but minimal fertilization is best as tall, top-heavy growth can cause plants to lodge, or fall over.

Harvesting

Amaranth keeps on flowering until hit by the first hard frost. Seed will often ripen many weeks before that, usually after about three months. The best way to determine if seed is harvestable is to gently but briskly shake or rub the flower heads between the hands and see if the seeds readily fall out. (Numerous small and appreciative birds may give you a hint as to when to start doing this.) There will be considerable variation between plants. An easy way to gather ripe grain is, in dry weather, to bend the plants over a bucket and rub the seedheads between the hands. Progressive maturation of seed will necessitate further threshing every week or so. (I have found that cutting and hanging plants to dry indoors does not work very well: the plants become extremely bristly and it is difficult to separate the seed from the chaff.) Clean the seed with screens, by winnowing, with a fan or other device. After harvesting, it is important to further dry your amaranth seed or it will quickly mold in storage. It can be left on trays in the hot sun to be stirred occasionally or placed near an indoor heat source until it is as dry as possible. Store dried amaranth in air-tight containers in a cool dry place.

The best time to harvest amaranth commercially is in dry weather three to seven days after frost—a condition not easily met in many places. Most presently available varieties maintain too high a moisture content to be harvested mechanically before a killing frost. The home gardener, however, can harvest ripe seed at any time with the caveat that further drying will always be necessary.

Normal commercial yields for amaranth are as yet the same as for quinoa—1200 to 2000 pounds (500-900 kg) per acre. As with quinoa, agricultural combines are still being adapted to the lightness of the seed, and full harvest potential is yet to be realized. Much higher results are obtained from labor-intensive harvesting: yields of over 5,000 pounds per acre have been reported from Central and South America.

Cooking Tips

Amaranth is a first-rate source of both grain and leaf protein. Its seed contains over 15 percent protein—more than any other grain except quinoa. The grain cooks up simply like quinoa, can be prepared in similar ways and is even more delicious. It is not covered by saponin so does not require any lengthy rinsing procedure. Amaranth seed is often ground into flour; it contains more gluten than that of quinoa and combines well with traditional flours in the ratio of one part amaranth to four parts other grains. Toasted and milled amaranth makes a hearty cooked cereal and some varieties can be popped like popcorn.

The leaves of amaranth are even more nutritious than those of quinoa, though they are not nearly as digestible when raw. The greens and stalks of plants that are thinned can be steamed or stir-fried for a delectable treat. They taste like spinach with a touch of horseradish and are best steamed, stir-fried or incorporated into curries or casseroles. They are higher in calcium and iron than just about any other vegetable. Some varieties have better greens than others and are usually so indicated in seed catalogues. One of the tastiest amaranths grown for greens is called tampala. Amaranth is also called Chinese spinach because of its popularity in that country.

Only quinoa comes closer than amaranth to supplying all the essential life-sustaining nutrients in one food.

POPPED AMARANTH

Popping is ideally accomplished in a well-seasoned wok, although an iron skillet will do. Pop a small amount at a time at medium heat. Work quickly, shaking the wok by hand or using a natural bristle pastry brush to move the seeds around. Remove the popped seeds immediately. If the seeds stick, the temperature is too high; if the seeds don't pop, it is too low. One tablespoon of uncooked seeds yields about three table-spoons of popped seeds.

Use popped amaranth as a cold breakfast cereal, as a dessert topping, or as breading meal.

Quinoa and amaranth have exciting possibilities for the home gardener looking for easy-to-grow, high-protein foods. They have higher food quality than our common grains such as wheat and oats, and they don't have hulls that have to be removed by machinery prior to cooking. These hardy crops also offer compelling possibilities for the farmer in the light (or gloom) of recent North American drought. From my own success with growing amaranth and quinoa over many years, I would say that the difficulties in cultivating and preparing these two grains are relatively minor and that the pleasures obtained in growing and eating them, are major. As we North Americans become familiar with these ancient plants, 5000-year friendships could easily develop.

6

A Gift For The Greening

Wanted: High-protein plant food usable in its natural state; suitable to large-scale farmers and home gardeners; adaptable to many climates and environments; ideally drought tolerant and soil enriching rather than depleting. Please reply as soon as possible to the hungry on ailing planet Earth.

Designer Plant

Imagine designing the perfect plant food to meet all of the above requirements. Can we hope for all of these attributes in one plant?

Such a plant does indeed exist and has been cultivated for over 5,000 years, most notably in China and Japan. Unfortunately, we have been missing the boat for most of this century, processing this wonderful legume in every imaginable fashion, instead of simply cooking it up! Most people have yet to discover the excellence of unadulterated soybeans. The wonder is that there are delicious soybean varieties that grow as easily as the indigestible ones you may have already tried and dismissed.

Soybeans are the largest crop in North America. Millions and millions of acres of soybeans are grown as fodder for cattle and pigs. The heavily subsidized meat and dairy industries wreak ecological havoc with both our water and soil resources. The question is, why grow soybeans to feed animals to feed people when we could be growing them to eat directly?

The reasons are embedded in the pervasive influence of the huge multinational corporations that control food production and agriculture as well as in deeply ingrained and scarcely examined cultural biases in dietary and eating patterns. Nevertheless, the notion of growing soybeans is rapidly eliciting accolades as one of the totally practical responses to our ecological crisis. We're growing soybeans on a huge scale already. It's just a matter of switching from the practically inedible varieties to those that make superlative human food when cooked as simply as other familiar beans.

Characteristics

Let's look at the attributes requested in the introductory advertisement for this designer power plant. Outside of considerations of taste, texture, color and differences in growth habits, the qualities of all soybean varieties are about the same. Soybeans are the only legume containing all nine essential amino acids (the only proteins the human body can't manufacture on its own). Soybeans have no cholesterol and are low in calories, saturated fats and sodium. They are an excellent source of dietary fibre. They are high in iron, calcium, B vitamins, zinc, lecithin, phosphorous and magnesium. However, it is important to note that a lot of this goodness is lost or diminished by processing soybeans. Tofu, for example, contains 28 percent less iron, only 10 percent of the fibre and B vitamins and none of the vitamins A and C found in cooked whole soybeans.

Despite the exaggeration of protein needs in North America, high-protein crops become more necessary as it becomes increasingly expensive and dangerous to eat at the top of the food chain. Commercial soybeans are relatively free of chemical toxins. Meat, fish and poultry have about twenty times and dairy foods about four and one half times more pesticide residues than soybeans. Similarly, soybeans contain fewer radioactive residues and no synthetic hormone additives.

Nutritional and health considerations aside, ecological factors figure as well in the choice of soybeans as a food. It is very evident that water will become a most precious resource in the coming decades, which makes the drought tolerance of soybeans a special asset. Nor are soybeans heavy feeders; they require minimal fertilizer and are nitrogen-fixing plants that enrich the soil. Also, the fact that soybeans can be simply cooked and eaten keeps energy output minimal. Freezing and canning are unnecessary, as are fancy plastic packages.

Global Hunger

The above attributes certainly argue strongly for soybeans to fill our bill. But consider also the following statistics in the soybeans portfolio.

Soybeans contain over 35 percent protein by weight—which is more than any other unprocessed plant or animal food. They produce over a third more protein from an acre of land than any other known crop. An acre of soybeans produces between ten and twenty times more useable protein than an equivalent acre used to graze beef cattle. The soybeans and grains that are currently being fed to livestock in North America could, if used for direct human consumption, make up for an estimated 90 percent of the world's protein deficiencies. In fact, if this were the case, only one-twentieth of these crops would be required for North American needs. The rest could go to the global food bank.

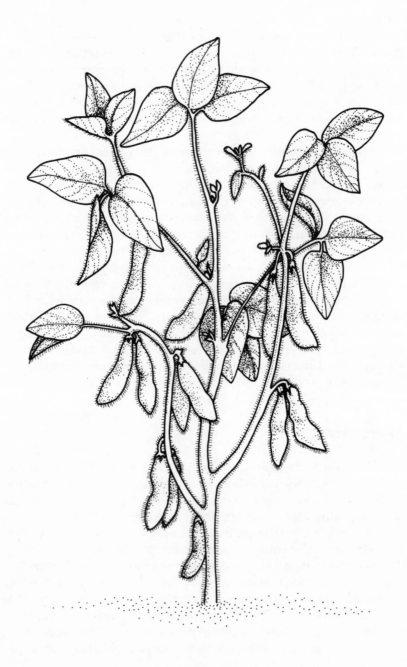

In 1987, I gave a bag of edible soybeans to a friend who was an agricultural advisor in Botswana. In early 1990, Gary informed me they were being grown enthusiastically in four or five countries in southern Africa—another indication that these jewels could help reduce global hunger!

Varieties

I have been popularizing a soybean variety called Black Jet for over eight years. In 1986, I started Salt Spring Seeds to formalize a process of mailing this variety to willing experimenters. Gardeners have been receptive to the point where recognition of Black Jets may now be approaching critical mass, at least in Canada. I feel that public enthusiasm for these soybeans might not take as long as it did for the tomato, which was thought to be poisonous for 300 years.

Black Jet soybeans take about four months to mature in the cool maritime climate of the Pacific Northwest but they mature in less than 100 days across much of the continent. One of my family's favorite dishes is tender black soybeans seasoned with a little garlic, ginger, molasses and cumin. A longer-season black soybean named Panther is reputedly even better-tasting, but that is hard to imagine. Johnny's of Albion, Maine carries it, as well as the Black Jets.

Since 1988, I've been growing another early-maturing soybean which I've named Grand Forks. These two-tone gold and brown soybeans look like kids' candies. A gourmet's delight, their buttery sweetness is enhanced by an herb and tomato sauce.

I've always had success with both the Black Jet and Grand Forks soybeans and have yet to experience any disease or pest problems. I usually plant in early May in rows about 1 1/2 feet (45 cm) apart. After a few weedings and hoeings the plants form an ample canopy that shades out weeds; there is nothing to do except water until harvest time in September. At times I've even grown soybeans with minimal irrigation and have still had a sizeable crop, probably because the roots grow deep to reach water.

The pea-shaped soybeans grow in two-inch (5-cm) pods with two to three beans per pod. Shelling the dry beans one by one can be tedious, but a circle of family or friends make it a harvest celebration. Over the years I've become adept at hand threshing piles of pods when they're brittle dry. A 200-foot (60-m) row will fill a gallon jar with about eight pounds (3.6 kg) of soybeans. Intensive raised beds can yield over four pounds per 36 square feet (2 kg per 4 square metres).

At this point, these exceptional soybeans are unavailable as food except to people who grow their own. But I think they present such a great advertisement for themselves that it won't be long before they're sold in supermarkets. The plants radiate a clean solidity, a robustness and a lushness which are consummated by the satisfaction of eating the cooked beans. They are a sustainable, delicious and totally appropriate food plant for our current and future sustenance. Try them, you'll love them!

7

Cool-Weather Legumes

Beans and soybeans, quinoa and amaranth luxuriate in the heat of the summer. There are other high-protein crops that thrive under cooler conditions and are normally harvested in July or August. Like these warm-weather crops, they are highly esteemed in many countries yet are almost unknown to North American farmers and gardeners.

Favas

Before 1990, I had often grown fava (or faba) beans as a cover crop. I appreciated their hardiness and nitrogen-fixing ability as well as the large quantity of green matter they add to the soil when turned under. I knew they had been a mainstay of the European diet until Columbus introduced warmer-weather beans. I also was aware that they had been grown by the ancient Egyptians and Chinese, as well as by the Greeks and Romans. Friends had told me that favas are a popular crop in India, Burma, Mexico and Brazil, and that they are eaten daily by millions of people in the Middle East. However, I had not considered fava beans a potential source of food for my family—we found the well-known Windsor Broad Bean passable in its fresh green state but unappealing as a dry bean. It wasn't until July 1990, after I'd begun testing other dry favas, when it dawned on me that people around the world eat them because they taste so good.

The fava is a member of the vetch family of the genus Vicia. It is a tall, upright annual with succulent-looking blue-green leaves on squarish and pulpy stalks that grow from four to five feet (120-150 cm) in most cultivars. Flowers are white with distinctive black centres and the pods that splay out from the stem vary considerably in length, some being up to a foot (30 cm) long. Some varieties have eight large, lima-sized seeds per pod. The pods have a very unusual white and fuzzy interior. As the plant dies down, the pods at the base of the stalk blacken first, then several weeks later all the pods will be black and dry.

In Their Favor

Fava beans are a tenacious and trouble-free crop that succeed where the growing season is short and other beans would fail—they survive temperatures as low as 6°F (-14°C). They require minimal or no watering as long as there are good spring rains. They are easy to grow and produce abundantly—yields of 3000 pounds (1360 kg) to the acre have been obtained in Saskatchewan. They add nitrogen to the soil and much humus when reincorporated. For the grower who has livestock to feed, they produce silage as valuable as that of alfalfa, field peas or grass/ legume hay, and the beans themselves are rich enough to replace the traditional soybean meal as a protein supplement.

In coastal and southern areas, favas can be planted in spring or fall; if planted in October or November, they serve a dual purpose as a winter cover crop and as a food plant.

Limitations

Most North American winters other than these latter are too cold for them to survive. Also,continental summers can be too hot for some varieties of favas because their blossoms will fall off before setting pods if temperatures go above 70°F (21°C). However, in most of the continent, the earliest possible planting in the spring will enable plants to mature beans. Strategies that prolong pea harvests also work for favas, such as planting in shadier areas, hilling up soil around the base of plants, mulching and keeping the soil moist.

A few individuals—usually males of Mediterranean descent—experience a hereditary allergic reaction when they eat fresh (rather than dried) beans or inhale fava pollen. The symptoms of "favism" usually disappear without treatment within a few days of exposure. Where fava beans are a dietary staple, allergies to them are detected as a matter of course; in North America, the possibility of allergic reaction, though extremely slight, is worth bearing in mind.

Growing Considerations

I have grown favas successfully in many different soils and have found that they thrive even in heavy clay. Being very vigorous, they shouldn't need fertilizer if grown in built-up garden soil. They do best in well-cultivated ground that is high in phosphorous and potassium and, like peas, they prefer soil that is not too acidic.

They are hardier than peas, so if you can plant out peas in autumn, you can plant out favas as well. In spring, they are generally seeded as soon as the soil can be worked—light frost will not harm the young plants. Soaking the seeds overnight ensures fast, even germination. In garden beds, the seeds should be planted one to two inches (2.5 to 5.0-cm) deep and four to six inches (10 to 15-cm) apart, in rows a foot or two (30 to 60 cm) apart. They compete poorly with weeds until they start to tower above them and, in the early stages, can benefit considerably with mulching or drawing soil around the base of the plants with a hoe or rake. (This latter process is called "earthing up" and is commonly done to potatoes.) Varieties I've tried so far haven't required support, but in windy places it might be worthwhile staking either end of the row and enclosing them with string.

Favas are fairly pest and disease resistant. Their most common problem seems to be aphids. Some writers suggest controlling aphid appearances by using insecticidal soap or by pinching off plant tops. Although I've seen a lot of aphids on my favas, I don't think they have affected the harvest.

Harvesting

Picked green as soon as the pods are well formed and deep green, favas can be eaten fresh or cooked. Farmers usually combine or cut field favas for silage when the two lowest pods have blackened, but the home gardener wanting dry beans can wait until half the pods have dried black—usually by the end of July. It takes several weeks for all the pods to dry, necessitating two or three pickings. The weather of late July and early August most often enables leisurely harvesting. When sufficiently dry, a fingernail won't dent the bean. They can be shelled by hand or threshed by foot in a box or on a tarp. If left standing too long in hot weather, the pods of some varieties will shatter and the beans fall to the ground.

Varieties

I have been researching the eating qualities of different cultivars. One I already find exceptional is called tic bean or bell bean. It stands out not only for its taste when cooked as a dry bean but also for its abundant yields of up to eight pounds (3.6 kg) per 50 feet (15 m). Growing four to five feet (120-150 cm) like most favas, it is an even hardier relative. The seed is more like a large, wrinkled pea rather than having the huge kidney shape of other favas.

My favorite of the large-seeded cultivars, which are often called broad or horse beans, is an unnamed one given to me by a friend, which I hope to make available when I have sufficient quantities. Other good varieties are Aquadulce Claudia sold by Territorial Seeds, Aprovecho carried by Abundant Life, Colossal by Vesey's and Toto which is sold by Stokes. (Check the sources in the bibliography.) Windsor, the most commonly available commercial variety, is not bad eating as a shell bean, but is thick-skinned and mealy when cooked as a dry bean.

Eating Favas

Writers point out that favas need a long soaking and many hours' cooking. I have found, though, that all the favas I've grown require only an hour's simmering after an overnight soak. The seedcoat retains a chewiness that is quite pleasant in some varieties but unpleasantly tough in others. The taste in the best varieties is rich, earthy and sweet, and easily the equal of any other bean.

Some writers recommend popping dried favas like popcorn or roasting them like peanuts.

The taste of fresh green favas stewed or simmered is somewhere between that of peas and limas. They are too old for fresh use if a yellowish green skin has already formed. As well, some varieties have a light green outer part that needs to be removed so that only the inner dark green part is eaten.

Green favas have as much protein as green limas, ten times as much as snap beans and about a quarter more than fresh peas, plus more iron and potassium than any of these. Dried favas average about 30 percent protein (compared to 40 percent for soybeans and 20-25 percent for most other dry beans); they contain very little oil but are high in carbohydrates.

In the Middle East, fava beans are traditionally prepared with lemon, olive oil and garlic, as in the following recipe.

FASALADA SOPA (Serves 3-4)

1	onion, sliced	
1	clove garlic, crushed	
3 Tbsp	olive oil	45 mL
1 Tbsp	tomato paste	15 mL
1/2 tsp	dried thyme	2.5 mL
1 cup	soaked fava beans	250 mL
	juice of 1 lemon	
	handful of chopped parsley	

Cook the onion and garlic gently in the oil until soft but not brown. Stir in the tomato paste and thyme. Add the beans and cook for 1 hour in enough water to cover by 1 inch (2.5 cm).

Sieve the mixture coarsely or puree in a blender at slow speed. Stir in the lemon juice and parsley. Serve hot.

Chick-peas

Chick-peas or garbanzos, as they're also known, have been grown in Mediterranean countries since as early as 8000 B.C. The Romans used the word *arietinum* (ram-like) to describe this bean because its roundish, compressed seed somewhat resembles a ram's head with horns curling over the sides. *Cicer arietnum* was a staple of their diet and still plays an important part in the regional cooking of southern Europe. Chick-peas are widely grown in India and Burma where they rival wheat in acreage under cultivation and are India's most important legume.

The chick-pea is a delicate, graceful plant which branches near the ground and is 20-inches to two-feet (50 to 60 cm) high. One or two seeds are borne in numerous round swollen pods about four months from the time of sowing.

In 1990 I discovered that garbanzos were not a warm-weather crop like lima beans but could be sown like peas early in spring. In 1991, all the seeds I sowed in early March came up, despite heavy nightly frosts. The plants are best thinned to about a foot (30 cm) apart because of their spreading habit. They don't need staking. They require little attention beyond the occasional weeding or hoeing and are quite drought tolerant. The dry pods are more difficult to process than those of other beans: the shells have a lanolin-like stickiness and cave in rather than split apart when hand-threshed. I recommend you place them on a tarp on the ground or in a large container such as a box or an ice chest and "do the shuffle" over them.

Chick-peas come in different colors but the black and green ones I've tried are quite insipid. The common light-beige garbanzo, however, has a rich, full flavor that makes it perfect for pâtés, casseroles and soups. My favorite by far, is a cultivar called Chestnut Chick-pea which I originally obtained from Dominion Seed House. If you've already prepared such specialty dishes as tabouli and humous, you're in for a special treat when you prepare them with homegrown garbanzos. As with other fresh-grown beans, cooking times are considerably less than what is usually recommended. In this case, 90 minutes is sufficient after an overnight soaking (rather than two and a half hours).

The chick-pea is one of the most nutritious members of the bean family—rich in protein, calcium, iron and B vitamins.

Loving Kindness Humous (Serves 6)

1 cup	chick-peas	250 mL
1	carrot, large	
3 or more	garlic cloves	
1	bay leaf	
2	lemons, juiced	
1/2 cup	sesame tahini	125 mL
5 or more	garlic cloves	
	salt to taste	

Soak chick-peas in 3 cups cold water for at least 4 hours. Rinse and add fresh water to cover. Boil for 1 1/2 hours with coarsely chopped carrot, whole peeled garlic cloves and bay leaf, until very tender. Drain, reserving cooking liquid.

Remove bay leaf and mash while still hot. Stir in the lemon juice, tahini, and crushed or finely chopped garlic. Add small amounts of cooking liquid until desired moistness is reached. Salt to taste.

Serve with whole-grain crackers or Arab (pita) bread as an appetizer or snack. Makes good lunch sandwiches too.

Lentils

Lentils have been cultivated for 10,000 or more years. *Lens* is the Latin word for lentil, hence its coinage in the seventeenth century as the word for a doubly convex piece of glass shaped like a lentil. Lentils are enormously important in many countries, especially in Asia and North Africa.

Lentils are a small and very branching plant, forming a tuft just over a foot (30 cm) high. The small white or pale blue flowers are produced in pairs and are succeeded by very flat pods, each of which usually contains two seeds. Lentils are closely related to peas and, like them, do

best in cool, moist, sandy loam. They are hardy, easy-to-grow nitrogen-fixers that can be planted as soon as the soil is workable in the spring. Sow the seeds about half an inch deep (1.25 cm) and four inches (10 cm) apart.

Lentils are easily threshed but keep better in the pods, so quantities are best threshed out as required.

Lentils need no soaking and cook relatively quickly—from 10 to 30 minutes, depending on variety. They must be watched because, unlike garbanzos, they soften easily and can lose their texture. In the Middle East they are most often used in soups and stews and are frequently flavored with lemon, olive oil and garlic. In south India, where they are a major source of protein, many methods are used to prepare lentils for breads, fritters, salads, pancakes and vegetable dishes. Lentils are 25 percent protein and are rich in iron and vitamin B.

Store-bought lentils have matured easily for me but yields were extremely low. However I obtained an excellent variety called horse lentils from Jim Ternier's seed company in Saskatchewan. Horse lentils are a very pretty plant, with finely divided leaves and blue flowers. They produce copious amounts of large, angular, grey-green lentils which are as delicious as any I've tasted.

Peas

Having written about favas, chick-peas and lentils, all of which are grown much like peas, it would be remiss of me not to mention peas themselves. Peas are another legume whose dry seeds can be stored without processing, until ready for use.

In 1990, I discovered several fine soup pea varieties that I hope to offer in the future, but my favorites continue to be two I've already listed in Salt Spring Seeds' catalogue. I originally obtained them from William Dam Seeds and they are Dutch cultivars called Capucijners after the Capucine monks who grew them. The shorter Capucijners don't need staking and have beautiful white and maroon flowers, while the taller Capucijners need support and have fragrant pink and burgundy blossoms that are replaced by purple pods. The wrinkled peas look like brown/green pebbles and cook up whole into a rich, brown gravy. Although I once thought peas couldn't be used for soup unless they were split, soup from these peas is now relished winter fare at our house. We've also had good soups from regular shell peas that were allowed to dry on the vine.

Favas, chick-peas, lentils and peas are beautiful plants that enrich the soil and require little care. Planted when soil moisture abounds, they are harvested when dry weather is expected. They provide year-round sustenance but store without packaging or processing. They are nourishing, versatile, simple foods that have been with us for centuries. Together with beans, soybeans, quinoa and amaranth, they offer diverse and rewarding choices to the home gardener looking for efficient, low-impact means to grow and consume food.

8

Ladies And Gentlemen: The Queens

Some food plants tower over others in their capacity to nourish and sustain us. Similarly, there are medicinal plants whose safe, yet powerful healing energy speaks for their inclusion in any garden that aims to reclaim local control of medicine and to optimize our well-being. Of all the healing herbs I grow, the two I value most highly are garlic and echinacea. I grow them for family and friends, for my seed company and as cash crops.

Echinacea

You may already be growing echinacea (*eck in ay see ah*) unawares in your garden as it is none other than Purple Coneflower—a striking ornamental that few flowers can match for elegance. Similarly, few perennials offer such a generous season of bloom and require such little care. *Echinacea purpurea* has been a popular garden plant for 200 years. Its fragrant flower has an spikey, conical, orange centre, surrounded by long and stately, purple ray florets falling graciously from it. The plant grows to four feet (1.2 m) tall and bears numerous flower stalks shooting up from a single root. The leaves are oval to broadly lance-shaped with irregular coarse teeth. Purple Coneflower is a late summer to fall bloomer that likes sun, withstands drought and is disease-free. Never insect-free, however, it attracts masses of harmless bumblebees and butterflies throughout its blooming season.

Medicinal Uses

"Echinacea—Number One Herb of the 90s" proclaims the recent cover of a national health magazine. Popularity and esteem are nothing new to this queenly herb. The most valued medicinal plant of the American plains natives, echinacea was widely known and used throughout North America until the shift to synthetic drugs after the first World War. Europeans have respected echinacea's healing power for several decades, and North Americans are now once again stocking it in their medicine cabinets. An abundance of scientific data indicates that it is potent, yet non-toxic. If you want to rely more on yourself and less on multinational corporations for your health and medicine, you would do well to grow this wonderful herb.

During the past four decades, scientific researchers have isolated many diverse and powerful chemical compounds in echinacea. Studies have basically validated traditional native healing uses for the plant. Echinacea is anti-inflammatory, has strong wound healing action and stimulates the immune system. It has a reputation as the most effective blood and lymphatic cleanser in the botanical kingdom. Useful for treating gangrene, venomous insect or animal bites and other kinds of blood poisoning, it is also effective for many chronic or acute bacterial

and viral infections. Researchers see great potential for using echinacea as a therapeutic agent in the treatment of diseases ranging from asthma to cancer. Not surprisingly, many pharmaceutical and herbal preparations—ointments, creams, lotions, fluid extracts and tinctures—contain echinacea.

For home use you can use the dried roots, leaves and/or seeds of echinacea in the standard proportion of one teaspoon per cup (5 ml per 240 ml) to make tea. Currently, the most popular way of taking echinacea, however, is as a tincture. While tinctures are usually alcohol-based, echinacea requires both alcohol and water because of the plant's unique chemistry. Echinacea contains giant sugar molecules, or polysaccharides, which are similar to bacterial cells. Best extracted by water, they activate the immune system and are completely non-toxic. The other agent, echinacein, is a pungent, anti-bacterial oil that is mostly alcohol-soluble. (If you have ever chewed the seeds or root of echinacea, or tried the tincture, you're familiar with the odd tingling and numbing sensation this causes.) Hence, the tincture is usually made with equal proportions of high-proof grain alcohol and distilled water. To prepare the tincture, combine finely-grated, chopped or macerated roots, seeds and/or leaves to the alcohol/water combination in the ratio of 3.5 ounces (100 gr) to 1.5 cups (350 ml). Shake the mixture daily for two weeks, strain, and filter into brown dropper bottles, available at pharmacies. It is common practice in some circles to process the tincture between the new and full moon.

Studies show that echinacea's effectiveness depends on taking enough, yet not too much. When you feel a cold or flu coming on, try a dropperful of the tincture three times a day. For an active disease state, it's important that the body maintain a certain level of the active components for maximum healing potency. As a result, one to three droppersful every two hours for seven to ten days is often prescribed. After ten days, effectiveness diminishes rapidly and a rest of five to seven days is advisable before taking echinacea again.

Despite considerable debate about which species of echinacea is best for medicinal use, research finds the common garden species, *Echinacea purpurea*, to be as effective as other species, such as *E. angustifolia* or *E. pallida*. Since Echinacea purpurea is widely available, and easy to propagate and grow, you need look no farther if you wish to use echinacea for home medicines.

Cultivation

Echinacea can be started from seed, by dividing offshoots of the crowns, or by planting four-inch to five-inch (10 to 12 cm) sections of the root. If you choose to start from seed, you can generally improve the speed and frequency of germination by putting fresh seeds in the freezer for one or two months. Some recommend putting the seeds in a bag of moist sand, vermiculite or sawdust before freezing, but I simply leave my seed jar outside in the cold. Subjecting seeds to freezing temperatures to boost germination is often called cold stratification. By the way, as I write, the seeds I am testing for Salt Spring Seeds have given me 60 percent germination without, and 90 percent germination with, stratification.

Although seeds can be sown directly in the spring, you'll have more success by starting transplants. The components of your soil mix aren't crucial but, because light hastens germination, it's best to place the seeds on top of the soil mix, then tamp them down on the surface.

Once young seedlings are six to seven weeks old, they're ready to transplant to permanent locations. Echinacea prefers a somewhat alkaline (pH of 6.0 or greater), well-drained soil in a sunny location, though it will tolerate some shade. Space plants from one and one half to two feet (45 to 60 cm) apart and keep weeds in check by shallow surface cultivation and/or mulching. No staking is required. This plant is remarkably drought-resistant, so should need little if any water unless there is an extended dry spell. Established plants are hardy and survive winters without attention.

Echinacea often flowers late the first year, but you're more likely to enjoy their wonderful display in subsequent seasons. The roots will be large enough to harvest for medicinal use after three years. By that time, there will be up to seven baby offshoots attached to the main root. You can multiply your stock by replanting these directly in the garden, but it's best to wait until fall, after the first few frosts.

All in all, echinacea combines aesthetic brilliance and precious usefulness. A regal addition to any perennial, cut-flower, native plant or informal garden, it is also one of our most potent herbal medicines. Echinacea will return your minimum care and attention with maximum enjoyment and healing.

Garlic

Garlic is justly famous for its gustatory delights and healing powers. It's amazing to me that despite how easy garlic is to grow, almost all the commercial garlic used in North America comes from California or Mexico. This garlic is usually of one variety, has been chemically treated, and is inferior to home-grown garlic in both taste and keeping qualities. It is for these reasons that I strongly encourage people to grow garlic for their own use, or even as a cash crop.

Cultural requirements for garlic are similar to those for onions, yet garlic always fetches ten times the market price of onions. The price of organically-grown garlic often exceeds four dollars per pound or nine dollars per kilogram, and a handsome braid of a dozen bulbs can easily cost $15. Besides the culinary and medicinal treasures it yields, even a small garlic plot can enable a grower to pay for garden inputs, such as rock phosphate or mulch hay. For serious enthusiasts, an acre of garlic can reap an $8,000 income, according to British Columbia agricultural officials. It seems timely to reduce the vast and unnecessary waste of non-renewable resources incurred by transporting garlic thousands of miles. I contend that if large, local plantations were set up to supply bioregions, it would cut the need for bulk imports and heighten regional sustainability.

Varieties

Without really planning to, I've found myself acquiring, growing and selling many different garlics. Most strains that have come to me have names of countries attached, such as Russian, French, Italian and Spanish garlic. I've even named a variety of unknown origin Salt Spring garlic, because it has been grown here for 16 years at Bright Farm. Varieties vary in height, size of cloves, ease of peeling and days to maturity. There are some non-bolting types, but most will send up a flower stalk when stressed by too much heat or too little water. The garlic best known to consumers has cloves clustered piggyback style in concentric layers with no central stalk. However some varieties, such as Chinese and Yugoslavian, have adjacent cloves against a thick central stalk.

Varieties also differ, as you might expect, in the pungency and texture of the cloves, especially when eaten raw. The discriminating raw garlic eater will find too that different varieties hit different parts of the tongue, or even the back of the throat, first! With cooked garlic, other varietal differences, such as degree of oiliness, are more noticeable.

As yet, there are no standards for identifying garlic varieties or strains. Those I've mentioned are classified as *Allium sativum*. There is also *Allium sativum ophioscordon*—Rocambole or serpent garlic: it always forms top bulbils as well as smallish underground bulbs and its stems grow in curious curls or knots. It can form a perennial patch. The small topsets can be used for flavor in cooking.

Elephant garlic, *Allium ampeloprasum*, is actually a giant leek and is also a perennial. Elephant garlic is milder then regular garlic but also has a characteristic bitterness when eaten raw. It is in great demand because of its excellent storage life and large size—some bulbs weigh over a pound (2.2 kg)!

Cultivation

Garlic is easy to cultivate and will do well in many types of soil. However, like its cousin, the onion, it appreciates rich, well-drained, sandy loam with plenty of humus. For poor and acidic (below 5.5 pH) soil, you'd do well to dig in compost or aged manure along with wood ashes, dolomite lime or crushed oyster shells. A caution, however against too rich a soil, which may cause the tops to overdevelop.

You may know that garlic repels some pests. For this reason, it is often recommended as a companion for roses, tomatoes and cabbages. You could therefore consider placing it appropriately in your garden— though never near asparagus or beans. (Note that used on plants as a spray, perhaps with cayenne for extra potency, garlic is usually effective against a variety of insects and is said to deter deer from nighttime foraging.)

Garlic can be planted in rows, double rows or intensive beds with five or six plants across. Choose a sunny location. To begin, break apart the bulbs without peeling any of the skin. Plant individual cloves, wide part down, about two inches (5 cm) deep so that the pointed end is slightly below the soil surface. The flat, grey-green leaves will grow on one- to three-foot (30 to 90 cm) stalks.

Although you can plant garlic anytime from August through spring, I favor a fall sowing, preferably in October or at least three to four weeks before the ground freezes. There are several reasons for this. For one, garlic needs at least a month of near-freezing temperatures, then a minimum of 100 days to mature. A fall sowing, especially in cold areas, allows the plants to get off to the earliest possible start in spring, which means a larger harvest. A mulch, which includes snow in cold climates, will help keep the cloves toasty during the winter. In maritime conditions, there is a lot of root growth during warm winter spells, causing leaves to shoot up several weeks before weeds in early spring.

Mulching material will also stem weed growth for awhile in the spring. Don't however, make the mistake I did one fall when I mulched with hay containing viable seed. It brought home to me how little garlic appreciates competition for light and nourishment: the garlic growing in grass had cloves half the size of those where the mulch behaved as it should. When it does come time to weed, if you don't continue mulching, practise shallow cultivation to avoid disturbing roots near the soil surface.

Other than weeding, garlic needs little care once it's planted. An occasional dose of fish fertilizer, available from garden shops, will likely boost leaf and bulb growth. Because most growth occurs before the summer sun starts to dry out the soil, garlic normally doesn't require much water—and never likes to be water-logged! To allow for optimum underground bulb-curing, avoid watering for a few weeks before harvest, which is usually around the end of July or early August. This often coincides with the time that your soil starts to dry to considerable depth anyway. If flower heads form at any time, cut them so that the plants put all their energy into bulb growth rather than seed formation. It makes a huge difference if you don't do this. I usually leave a few plants to flower each year and find their bulbs are always a quarter the size of their clipped neighbors'. If garlic does flower, the bulbils or "seeds" that may later form in clusters of four to 75 at the top of the stalk can be used as an alternate way of perpetuating your crop. Bulbils planted in the fall of one year develop small, undivided bulbs or bulbs of tiny cloves by the next fall. These must be dug and replanted to produce full-sized bulbs in the following year.

Harvesting and Storage

Though most garlic matures by early August, plants started from store-bought garlic may mature later in September the first year. The best time to harvest garlic is when at least half of the foliage has turned yellow. Stalks of some varieties will fall over when mature. Others can be knocked over, as you would with onions, to speed maturity. For the same reason, some growers recommend twisting the stem either before or after harvesting. If well-mulched, plants can be pulled easily by hand. Otherwise, dig them up carefully to avoid puncturing.

Some sources suggest bringing harvested garlic immediately under cover. Most, however, recommend you cure it in the sun for two days to two weeks, bringing it in or covering it if dew or rain threatens. For years, I always left my harvest outside for several days and had good success with storage and later germination. One year, fearful of rain, I brought my garlic immediately under cover, which proved to be a mistake as 10 percent of the bulbs had mold on them within a month. A word of caution, however: midsummer temperatures anywhere but near the coast might be too hot for garlic bulbs to be left spread on the ground for more than three or four days.

To store, remove by hand any dirt sticking to the bulbs, but leave intact as much skin as possible. Garlic plants with pliant stalks can be braided or otherwise hung in bunches. Alternately, cut the bulbs off, leaving an inch (2.5 cm) of the top and a half inch (1.25 cm) of root on each bulb. Don't store your bulbs in a refrigerator—the cold will cause cloves to sprout, which changes their flavor and texture. Generally speaking, a cool, airy place is the safest bet for winterkeeping, though you can expect some varieties to soften or shrivel before the next year's harvest. The cloves on good bulbs will be held together neatly by a white, pinkish or brownish, paper-thin skin. Use bruised, punctured, exposed or otherwise suspect cloves first. Save the biggest cloves from your biggest bulbs for planting, which you can do almost at once. Hopefully the cloves you save for eating will last until the next summer's crop!

If you have planted Elephant garlic, a couple of special notes apply. Because it's a perennial, it can be left in place all year. It's best however, to dig up the bulbs, separate the cloves and replant them as above. Also, unlike ordinary garlic, the cloves split up when dry, so it can't be hung indefinitely.

Uses

A tremendous amount of folklore attests to garlic's importance in many cultures. In the days of the pyramids, Egyptian slaves went on strike when garlic was withheld from their diet and the ordinary citizen swore on a clove of garlic when taking a solemn oath. Roman soldiers, who ate large quantities of garlic to give them strength and courage in battle, planted it in every country they conquered. (This was least appreciated by the British!) Even today, many folk staunchly maintain that vampires and werewolves will exit *toute de suite* when confronted with garlic's odiferous presence.

Folklore related to garlic's medicinal value abounds as well. The Chinese have revered it for at least 6000 years for its ability to fight infection, promote healing and aid digestion. An Egyptian medical listing, dated around 1500 B.C., recommends it as a remedy for 22 problems. Pliny the Roman claimed it effective in treating 61 ailments!

Modern research has corroborated many of these claims. Garlic has proven effective in reducing high blood pressure, inhibiting malignant tumors and easing respiratory problems. Research also confirms its efficacy as an antiseptic and an insecticide. Some health practitioners, though, warn against garlic's excessive heat-producing qualities.

Allicin is the ingredient that both gives garlic its odor and destroys or inhibits various bacteria, fungi and yeasts. Allicin forms when the cloves are crushed but is destroyed on cooking. It is doubtful, therefore, whether odorless or cooked garlic has much medicinal value. Many cooks, in recognition of this principle, add finely-chopped cloves to hot dishes just minutes before serving.

Nonetheless, you'd be hard-pressed to find a cookbook that doesn't mention garlic. It is celebrated in cuisines the world over and is appropriate to virtually any food except desserts. Garlic's pungent, appetizing flavor blends with other flavors nicely and is mellowed by long, moist stewing. (Note that garlic becomes bitter if burnt—an undesirable effect in all but a special cuisine called Neapolitan.)

There are a multitude of ways to use garlic, but here are a few my family particularly loves.

Recipes

Roasted garlic: Roast unpeeled cloves for 15 minutes in a medium oven. Peel and mash to use in sauces, purées, soups and marinades. Roasting gives garlic a mild, nutty flavor.

Salad dressing: Crush five to ten garlic cloves with the broad side of a stainless steel knife. Peel, then place them in a quart or liter of olive oil for a week. Store at room temperature, shaking occasionally. Combine with herbed vinegar and mustard as the basis of a salad dressing. Refrigerate.

Garlic vinegar: Peel a clove of garlic and let it sit in a small container of vinegar for three to four days.

Pesto sauce: Combine garlic, pine nuts (substitute: walnuts, almonds or sunflower seeds) and onion with basil, parsley, Parmesan cheese and olive oil. (Instead of basil, try dill, chervil, summer savory, lovage or cilantro.) This is a wonderful sauce over pasta or potatoes that's all the rage these days.

Garlic greens: Consider growing a small patch of garlic exclusively for greens. Garlic greens can be chopped and added to salads, soups and omelets throughout the growing season.

Remedy for garlic breath? Most recommend you eat a sprig of parsley. Or, stay in the company of other garlic lovers!

As we green the garden, many plants are candidates for becoming part of the living medicine chest that can exist right outside our doors. As we shall see in the next chapter, many native wild plants are actually wonderful healing herbs that we can cultivate in our gardens. Few however, surpass echinacea and garlic for their potency, majesty, hardiness and ease of cultivation.

9

Weeds, Please!

The gardener looking to sustainability goes beyond the management practices of the conventional organic gardener and does not think of all weeds as intruders. Many locally-adapted plants can be as useful as gardener-initiated ones and can enhance our ability to provide for ourselves with their culinary and medicinal properties. A lot of gardeners like to have immaculately-weeded gardens, but I say let's conserve patches of immaculate weeds! If you welcome some of them, I'm sure you'll be glad of their acquaintance.

My Favorites

Many pretty and useful wild plants appreciate the optimum conditions we gardeners give to our sprouting seeds. Most weeds want only a little elbow room. In return, they'll add heartiness to soups, zest to salads and healing power to teas. Some will keep soil cool, moist and in fine tilth; some will bring up minerals from the sub-soil; some will delight you with their sparkling flowers.

I give as much thought to where I'll leave, undisturbed, those garden weeds that I value for food and medicine as I do to my herbs and vegetables. In selected places, I allow to flourish about a dozen familiar weeds which I regard as respected garden companions.

Chickweed

There are several kinds of chickweed, but my favorite is the most common, *Stellaria media*. A resident of most garden beds, it forms a mat-like growth from three inches to a foot (7.5 to 30 cm) high and has a line of hairs running up one side of the stem. It flowers in early spring in small white, leafy clusters. One plant can cover many feet in area, forming an effective mulch that conserves moisture and chokes other weeds. (If you do weed chickweed or harvest an entire plant, it's quite the thrill to see large, clear soil areas manifest with only a yank or two.)

Because it is one of my favorite salad greens, I usually let chickweed thrive in a few of the moist places it likes. I clip off straggly growth and sometimes even fertilize it with manure or compost tea. Once one becomes familiar with chickweed's growing habits, its lush growth becomes a good indicator of high nitrogen levels in the soil.

Although gardeners are often irritated by chickweed, it is more nutritious than most vegetables from which you might try to protect it. It is very high in copper and iron. Chickweed can be cooked in soups, casseroles and other dishes but its cool, soothing taste is best enjoyed raw in salads or munched fresh by itself. It seldom gets tough or fibrous with age and can be picked until snowfall, if not year-round, especially near sea level.

Chickweed is justly famous for its healing properties, so you'll find chickweed ointments and salves in pharmacies and herbal stores. It draws and absorbs infections and impurities from skin sores and wounds. Fresh from the garden, you can wash and apply the herb directly to the surface and hold it in place with bandages. It should be applied fresh every few hours. Chickweed tea or infusion (the proper name for an herb soaked in hot water) is equally soothing for internal inflammations, especially digestive upsets and for sore chest, lungs and throat. It can be made stronger than the usual teaspoon of dry herb per cup of water. If you have a lot of chickweed within easy access, put several handfuls in your next bath and acquaint yourself with the pleasure of a chickweed soak.

Cress

Another frequent inhabitant of moist garden spots, this plant is also known as rock cress. A miniature cousin of watercress, it has opposite oval-pointed leaves with one leaf on the end of the stalk. Like its frequent friend, lemon-tasting sheep sorrel, it makes for an enjoyable garden nibble and is chock-full of vitamins and minerals. Although only a little plant, it takes only a bit of its leaves' peppery taste to effectively spice up soups and salads. Cress self-sows readily, but poses little threat to other plants and helps prevent surface evaporation.

Burdock

This is the plant that helps you remember where you were last by leaving its sticky burrs on you. It has a thick stem with many branches and bristly, purplish flowers. The leaves are very large and woolly underneath. Burdock can be controlled by cutting it down before flowering. Baby burdocks take a while to develop a deep root and are easily weeded out.

What makes this plant special for me is the delicious, full-bodied tea made from its roots. So, believe it or not, I'm always happy to see burdock growing in my gardens and sometimes plant it deliberately. It is so much easier to dig burdock roots from garden soil: they grow straight and even like carrots and don't break off as they do in the compacted ground of upland or roadside. You can use either fresh or dried roots for tea, which is more like a broth or coffee, needing no sugar or cream to satisfy the taste buds. They are usually harvested in the fall. After cleaning, they can be cut in small pieces, a tablespoon per cup of water, before bringing them to a boil and simmering. I cut fresh burdock roots in fine slivers (much harder to do once the root starts to dry) and roast them gently in an oven. A teaspoon of the dry roasted root, simmered for five to ten minutes in a cup of water is about right. Burdock is very high in iron as well as in a sugar called inulin and many herbalists consider it a superb blood purifier. Burdock tea is therefore wonderful to take during a fast or at the first sign of skin eruptions.

In Japan and Quebec, a kind of burdock is grown which is popularly used in stews. It is usually three feet (1 m) or so long and the thickness of a medium-size carrot.

Yarrow

There are many cultivated varieties of yarrow but, to my mind, the wild plant is as beautiful as any of them. A perennial, its finely-divided leaves resemble large, fuzzy pipe cleaners and run along a hairy stem. Its fragrant white flowers bloom most of the summer, so be sure to let a few plants flourish. You'll enjoy not only their fragrance, but also looking at the dense mass of white that the small, numerous flower heads form.

Yarrow tea's peppery, sage-like taste is something you'll enjoy as well. Made from both leaves and flowers, it has a purifying and uplifting effect as an occasional tonic. A strong infusion of yarrow tea is great for fevers as it dilates skin pores to produce copious sweating. An alternate remedy for the same purpose is to toss a few handfuls of leaves into a bath. In addition, both tooth-ache and earache can be relieved by yarrow. Its aromatic essence produces an anaesthetic effect similar to freezing. So, the next time you have a toothache, chew a few yarrow leaves! For earache, place a wad of warmed, crushed leaves or a few drops of strong tea in the affected ear.

An infusion of yarrow leaves makes a fine hair rinse as well. Steep a quantity of the fresh or dried herb in boiled water, perhaps along with chamomile or nettle. Add a few squirts of cider vinegar or lemon and let cool to the preferred temperature before using.

Nettle

A valuable plant, nettle is among the most painful to weed! In fact, most people know nettles from their small, stinging barbs and are put off eating them for the same reason. But if you gather the tops with gloves (I usually snip them with scissors) and steam them for a few minutes in their own moisture, they are fantastic and there is no stinging effect at all.

Nettles are rare in gardens with good sun exposure as they need cooler, somewhat shaded areas to get established. Stands of nettle most often occur on the edges of gardens, under trees or beside buildings. A patch of nettles will gradually spread out through root growth and should be cut back when it becomes invasive. As with burdock, this "weed" can also be controlled by not allowing it to flower.

Early spring, when the paired leaves are often tinged a beautiful violet, is the best harvesting time. If you keep cutting them in fact, they'll continue to give you choice top growth. However, if you let them go until the beginning of summer, drooping flower clusters begin to form. Once mature, nettle leaves aren't nearly as delectable but can still be used to make tea. For me, the special delight of nettles is cooking and eating those first luscious, mauve-green leaves. That's when I know spring has arrived!

Early nettles can also provide that much-needed spring tonic. They are rich in vitamins A and C, chlorophyll, iron and calcium, and are one of the few plants to contain vitamin D, which is necessary for calcium assimilation and bone development. Nettle is thus an excellent herb to

take for anemia and other blood conditions. Nettle tea is soothing and healing when you have a burn, hives, hemorrhoids or sore kidneys. Applying fresh nettles (that's deliberately stinging yourself!) to many kinds of skin rash and to rheumatic joints will usually bring great relief: the stinging stimulates the body's flow of blood and production of cortisone.

Nettle has an abundance of other uses. Massaging the scalp with a strong tea infusion or using it as a hair rinse after shampooing will improve the color and texture of the hair and remove dandruff. The roots yield a yellow dye and boiling the plant with salt produces a liquor that can substitute for rennet.

If you do get stung by nettles, look for dock, which almost always grows nearby. The juice from the bruised leaves, rubbed on the affected area, soothes the stinging pain for most people.

Dock

Dock, also known as Curled or Yellow Dock, not only relieves nettle stings, but is a good medicinal plant. I usually let some dock grow to maturity in my gardens but keep it mostly out of sight because of its somewhat motley appearance. Its large basal, triangular leaves curl at the edges and often have reddish veins. It grows to about three feet (90 cm) and its small greenish flowers are crowded in long, terminal clusters that redden as the fruit ripens.

Young dock leaves have a rhubarb taste with a slight lemony tang. For lemon flavor, I actually prefer dock's tiny cousin, *Rumex acetosella*, or sheep sorrel. Its arrow-shaped, sour-tasting leaves are always a favorite of children, making it another weed to appreciate.

The root of dock (normally dug in autumn) makes a potent nutritive tonic and astringent purifier, useful in treating blood problems and skin ailments. It stimulates digestion, improves stomach and liver function and stimulates elimination by improving the flow of bile and acting as a laxative.

Dock tea is prepared by simmering a teaspoonful of the dried root per cup of water for five to ten minutes.

Miner's Lettuce

This plant often crops up in garden beds and ranks among the finest salad greens of the wild edibles. It certainly can't be classified as a troublesome weed and is worth saving and harvesting for an extra salad treat. There are two species of miner's lettuce. *Montia perfoliata* has saucer-shaped upper leaves through which the stem protrudes. Its small, white flowers grow from stems arising from the centre of the leaf disks. *Montia sibirica*, or Siberian miner's lettuce, has short-stemmed upper leaves. Its flowers, on long thin stems, have five notched petals bearing thin red lines. Both of these plants flourish in moisture and shade.

The leaves of Siberian miner's lettuce are best eaten in early spring because they get bitter with age. Leaves of *M. perfoliata* can be eaten through summer and fall. If you boil the leaves and stems, take care not to over-cook these flavorful greens: a few minutes is sufficient.

Chicory

A common roadside plant, chicory is easily identified in mid-summer when it flowers in brilliant blue, dandelion-like heads. It has long, wiry stems and leaves similar to the dandelion at the base of the plant. It has appeared quite often in my gardens where I've planted yellow flowers nearby to highlight its warm azure color.

Young chicory leaves and shoots are good in salads and as a pot herb, especially when blanched to remove the slight bitterness. (To blanch, simply keep the plant out of direct sunlight for a few days.) The white underground parts of the leaves are quite succulent when dug out in spring. Specialty seed catalogues are featuring cultivated varieties of chicory such as radicchio these days.

For me, apart from its pretty flower, this plant's chief recommendation is the use of its roots for a beverage. And it is infinitely easier digging chicory roots from friable garden soil than the dry, hard-packed ground where it usually grows. The roots, harvested in fall, can be sliced, roasted and ground, or they can be freshly cut in small pieces then simmered. Like dandelion roots, they have a beneficial effect on the stomach, kidneys and liver. Combined, the roots of these two plants make a delicious, full-bodied tea. They also merge well with burdock root.

Dandelion

Not only does dandelion have a beautiful flower, but it is also an excellent food and medicinal plant. The young leaves, much higher in vitamins and minerals than the ordinary garden vegetable, can be used in salads, steamed briefly or cooked in soup. Cutting the leaves in small pieces before tossing them in salads helps tone their somewhat strong taste. Dried leaves can be used for teas or for making herb beer, and dandelion wine can be prepared from the flowers. The crown of blanched leaf stems on top of the root (the white part at the base of the leaves) is eating esteemed by many epicures, and the young roots can be cooked as a vegetable.

With its large supply of nutritive salts, dandelion is a blood tonic and stimulant for the entire system. It has a pronounced energizing effect on the stomach, liver, pancreas, kidneys and bowels. Dandelion root contains more of its active principles—taraxacin and inulin—in the autumn, but it is usually easiest to gather in the spring when the plant is most visible. With our oft-times extended Indian summers on the west coast, a second harvesting is usually possible, thanks to the seeds that were parachuting around in the spring. It's always best to gather dandelion leaves before the flower stalks appear.

To make dandelion coffee, dry, roast and grind the roots, then simmer them for five to ten minutes. Freshly sliced roots can be similarly simmered to make a full-bodied tea.

Clover

A familiar wayside and garden plant, clover can be either white or red. Some varieties are planted as a cover crop or green manure and some gardeners employ clover as a living mulch. Leaves and flowers of both white and red clover are high in protein and are edible raw or cooked, though it's best to soak them in salt water to render them more digestible. The reason I don't weed out all the red garden clover is that I prefer to be able to harvest fat, juicy blossoms with which to adorn the occasional salad. Two or three blossoms per person are about right.

Vitamin-rich red clover tea can be prepared by simple infusion: place the leaves and flowers in water and bring to the boiling point, or pour boiled water over them. Besides being delicious, clover tea is another good brew for internal cleansing. As well, it is good for coughs, colds and bronchitis. An excellent cough syrup can be made by straining a steeped infusion of clover blossoms, onion juice and warm honey.

Mullein

Like clover, mullein is often recommended for coughs and sore throats as well as lung and chest complaints. Seed companies specializing in flowers offer different varieties of mullein but, to my mind, the common wild plant has a stately elegance equal to any of them.

Mullein's large velvety leaves are like hairy blotting paper and are often over a foot long. Being a biennial, it will only flower in its second year. The flower stem is topped by a long spike of individual yellow flowers, usually blooming a few at a time from July on. If you decide to let a few mullein plants reach maturity, be sure they're in the center or back of the bed because these flower spikes can tower over you. Because it self-sows vigorously, be sure to cut mullein down early if you don't want it growing in the garden year after year.

A tea of dried mullein leaves (one teaspoon per cup) will usually bring relief from hay fever, asthma, bronchitis, coughs and congestion. Inhaling the steam from mullein or gargling the tea are equally effective. For external swelling or inflammation, soak a cloth in a hot and strong brew of the leaves or flowers, wring it out and apply directly. Dried mullein leaves, mixed with a little mint or sage, make a mild and satisfying herbal tobacco for those trying to break their addiction to nicotine.

Oregon Grape

Also known as Berberis or Mahonia, Oregon grape is an evergreen shrub that offers shiny holly-like foliage, clusters of fragrant yellow flowers and deep purple berries. It is common in coniferous forests of the east and west coasts of Canada and the northern U.S. and is found also in pastures, thickets and along roadsides. Because of its hardiness and attractiveness, Oregon grape makes a wonderful addition to a garden landscape. The fragrance of its flowers is exceptional and its leathery, lustrous leaves turn bronze, gold, crimson and purple in the fall. The leaves have prickly edges however, so it's best to keep Oregon grape in low maintenance areas.

Herbalists are most impressed with the part of Oregon grape that grows out of sight. Early settlers learned of the healing properties of this bitter-tasting root from native Americans and it was listed in official pharmacopoeias until 1950. The active ingredient that makes Oregon grape root such an effective remedy is an alkaloid called berberine. (This constituent is also found in other powerful healing herbs such as goldenseal.) Berberine stimulates bile secretion to promote good liver function and purifies the spleen and blood. Oregon grape root is a tonic for all the glands; its antiseptic effect is useful in douches and mouthwashes, and it is good for bronchial congestion. A tincture of Oregon grape is used to treat skin disorders such as eczema, acne and psoriasis.

The berries of Oregon grape have a slightly bitter but not unappetizing taste. They can be eaten raw or used to make jam, jelly or wine. They are sweeter after the first frost.

Shepherd's-purse

Another valuable garden weed, this plant gets its name from the purse-shaped seed pods along the stem. There is a round of dandelion-like leaves at the base, and the flowers, in terminal clusters, are small and white. It prefers open ground, and if you have it already, you're unlikely to get rid of it.

Though seeds and young leaves have edible uses, I usually just pick and dry shepherd's-purse leaves once in the spring. Besides containing large amounts of vitamins A and C, calcium, sodium and sulphur, shepherd's-purse is extremely high in vitamin K, the blood-clotting vitamin. Shepherd's-purse tea is therefore excellent for internal hemorrhages and a great one to have available for birthing moms.

Poultices made from fresh leaves, ointments and washes of shepherd's-purse serve well for external wounds.

Lamb's-quarters

Yet another tasty and nutritious garden weed, this plant is popularly known as pigweed and is found in almost any dry field at low elevation where the soil has been turned. You'll remember it as a cousin of quinoa. The diamond-shaped, dark green leaves radiate from the stem in four directions when young, and branch into more directions as they grow. If allowed to grow, it will reach two or more feet (60 cm) in height.

Lamb's-quarters can be used raw in salads or briefly cooked. The younger the leaves the better but this factor isn't as critical as it is for dock and dandelion leaves. Leaves from lamb's-quarters are enjoyably edible for many weeks and are very high in vitamins A and C. Their high oxalic acid content is mostly neutralized by a similarly high calcium content. Still, it is probably wise to avoid eating a great quantity at any one time. When juicing carrots or beets, try adding a small amount of pigweed leaves—about ten percent—for an especially potent punch.

Bruised and applied to the forehead, pigweed leaves are excellent for removing heat caused by a headache or too much sun.

Herbal Remedies

As noted in some of the above descriptions, the medicinal properties of almost any plant can be extracted by steeping a teaspoon (5 mL) of dried or fresh plant parts (i.e. leaves, flowers, stems and stalks) in a cup (240 mL) of boiling water for five to ten minutes. Generally speaking, the harder the plant parts, the more steeping is required. In fact, for roots alone, boiling them in the water and/or steeping them for a longer period, up to 20 or 30 minutes, is most effective. Another way of imbibing the healing properties of the roots of such plants as dandelion, chicory, Oregon grape, burdock and dock, is to make tinctures.

Tinctures

An herbal tincture is a highly concentrated plant extract that can be kept for long periods of time. It is a particularly efficient way of taking the blood purifiers and the liver and kidney tonics noted above because the alcohol used in preparation extracts all important ingredients. Herbs can be prepared alone or in combination.

Making a tincture is quite simple: the general formula is to combine four ounces (120 mL) of the powdered or cut herb with one pint (470 mL) of alcohol, such as vodka, brandy, gin or rum. Shake daily, allowing the herb to extract for about two weeks. (New moon to full moon is recommended.) Let the herb settle and pour off the tincture, straining out the powder or herb pieces through a fine cloth or filter. I usually put my completed tinctures in dark dropper bottles which are available from any drug store. The usual dose is five or six drops in a glass of juice or water once a day.

Well, in describing my favorite weeds, I've ended up with a gardener's dozen! To me, they offer an uplifting contrast to highly promoted consumer items. Lush salad greens touted by glossy seed catalogues frequently require just the right conditions for proper growth. Medicines in drugstores usually warn of possible side effects from their multisyllable ingredients. Herbal health remedies so often carry price tags commensurate with their exotic origins. But these weeds are nutritious foods and simple, safe medicines that are present for the taking throughout most of North America. I hope some of them give you as much joy and delight, healing and health as they do to me, my family and friends.

10

Friends Or Foes. . . ?

Sunroot and comfrey, while the bane of many gardeners, are welcomed as permanent companions in my gardens. They will not appear in the garden unless introduced, but once established, their robust appearance immediately attracts the eye. Both vigorous growers, they have the potential to become self-inflicted weeds, but gardeners can use this lush growth as superior compost and mulch material. Sunroot, also known as Jerusalem artichoke and as sunchoke, is an excellent food crop; comfrey has both medicinal and edible uses. The many benefits of these two plants can help us direct our gardening efforts toward more sustainable lifestyles.

Sunroot

Early in the seventeenth century, Samuel de Champlain found North American natives eating what they called "sunroots." These tubers not only became a staple winter food for early settlers, but also gained quick popularity in Europe. Its cultivation as a food crop throughout the western world faded, except in England, with the widespread introduction of potatoes in the following century. How did this plant come to be known as Jerusalem artichoke? It is thought that "Jerusalem" is a corruption of the Italian name for the plant, *girasole*, which refers to the plant's habit of turning its tall, sunflower-topped stalks toward the sun. The word "artichoke" was likely introduced because of the tuber's similarity in taste to globe artichokes. So, since it is neither from Jerusalem nor an artichoke, but a second cousin to the sunflower, let's do this plant a favor and call it sunroot. Its recent use in the production of ethanol has helped its public profile, and now that some seed companies are using its original name, it appears that this native perennial is destined for a well-deserved resurgence in popularity.

Pros and Cons

Sunroots are completely hardy, practically immune to pests and disease and unbothered by drought. They quickly grow bigger and tougher than weeds and can be left in the ground all winter to be dug up as needed. This plant can yield three to four times the harvest of potatoes and is capable of yielding twenty tons to the acre.

Sunroot's biggest drawback is its invasiveness. Its root system spreads far and wide from the main stem, forming the tubers that will produce new plants the following year. In fact, almost any fragment of a tuber will eventually send out a sprout. A small patch of these plants may, in a few years, become a very large patch with others appearing all over the place. My experience in harvesting sunroots is that you never dig them all. Furthermore, when dug, they seem to always piggyback to new territory by mischievous means. Short of bringing in a few pigs to root them out, you'll always have sunroots once you put them in the ground. (For hundreds of years in England and France artichokes one year for pigs to forage the next.)

New varieties have been developed that are less invasive and easier to clean. There are now long, yam-like types as well as shorter, smooth, carrot-like varieties. Unfortunately, these are not yet widely available, but seed companies should start to offer them soon.

In the meantime, I believe any gardener with a little extra space should consider trying our native sunroot. I wouldn't say it's impossible to contain the old varieties, but I would recommend isolating them in the garden or finding a spot for them outside your established plot. Unless, of course, you don't mind a few stalks popping up here and there, or the occasional challenge of removing uninvited stalks from unwanted places.

Cultivation and Harvest

Yes, sunroot will grow no matter how or where you plant it, but you can certainly help establish it by adding and digging humus-rich soil to a depth of at least six inches (15 cm). Its seed tubers are planted like potatoes, but you don't have to look for "eyes." Use whole tubers or cut them in chunks and plant them two to three inches (5.0 to 7.5 cm) deep and about a foot (30 cm) apart. Consider placing them to form an efficient screen for shade-loving plants or to hide a compost heap. (Cuttings of the fast-growing stalks are great for aerating compost when crisscrossed in the occasional layer.) They are also frequently planted in blocks along a north fence to make an effective windbreak. No matter where you plant them, they'll flourish!

Once planted, shoots will appear in three to four weeks. One weeding may be in order when the sprouts are about six inches (15 cm) high. After that, they'll take care of themselves and shoot skyward, like sunflowers, reaching six to twelve feet (1.8 to 3.6 m) in height, topped with yellow, daisy-like blossoms in the fall.

The tubers start forming with the onset of cold weather in September or October and keep growing after the visible plant has blackened and died. It's best, then, to wait until October or later to start harvesting. Sunroots are most delicious after the first frosts hit them and remain so until sprouting begins in spring. In most cases, a thick layer of mulch will help keep the ground soft enough to dig. It is best to start digging inwards at over a foot (30 cm) beyond the stalk to avoid mutilating the tubers, which grow on lateral shoots. You can expect about a pound (half a kilo) of tubers per plant. Sunroots are tricky to store because their thin skin causes them to shrivel easily. Simply leave them in the ground until you want to use them.

Culinary Uses

Sunroots store carbohydrates in the form of inulin instead of starch. As with most fruits, their sugars are stored as levulose. For these reasons, and because they have only one tenth the calories of white potatoes, they are often recommended for diabetics or anyone who needs to watch starch or calorie consumption.

After digging, use sunroots immediately or store, dirt intact, in the fridge. To prepare, clean them with a stiff brush under running water. Knobby parts can be cut to get into crevices if desired, but peeling is unnecessary. Because they discolor quickly, like apples, rub them with lemon juice or place them in cold water to which lemon juice or vinegar has been added, especially if there is a time gap between preparation and eating or cooking.

Sunroots have a unique sweet, nutty taste and crisp texture. They can be eaten raw, alone, or in salads. They also make a fine salad addition after light cooking. Add them to soups, or feature them in a cream soup. They can be steamed, sautéed or stir-fried, and cooked in most ways potatoes are prepared. Unlike potatoes, though, they lose a lot of their appeal when overcooked: five minutes of boiling is about right, or bake them in a fairly hot oven for about 15 minutes. Sunroots are delicious when they are boiled briefly, sliced and sautéed until golden brown then topped with parsley, chives or other herbs. Sunroot pickles are worth trying too: slice cleaned tubers thinly and marinate in your finest vinegar for at least a few days.

Comfrey

Comfrey's large, beautifully-veined, deep-green leaves grow in clumps that dominate their locale with elegance and beauty. Despite graceful appearances however, the leaves are covered with rough hair that can cause itching. The leaves decrease in length from over a foot to just a few inches long as they grow up the stem. In full sun or partial shade, comfrey grows two to four feet high and unfurls a succession of small yellow, mauve, blue or pink-white bells of flowers throughout summer. The plant dies back in cold weather but comes back strong in the spring and can last for a dozen years in the low, moist ground it prefers. Comfrey's thick rhizomes, which contain a fleshy and juicy mucilaginous substance, are black on the outside and white within.

Cultivation

The usual manner of propagating comfrey is to divide the roots in spring. A small piece of root will reproduce itself in any moist area in a very short time. Choose your location carefully because comfrey is a tough plant to get rid of once established. (In other words, never use comfrey as a cover crop!) Comfrey can be used to advantage as a background plant or screen. Although it will grow in almost any type of soil, it thrives in a damp location. Root pieces and offsets are best planted a few feet (over half a metre) apart and any soil amendments can only help comfrey to assert itself quickly. Annual removal of root offsets can keep your comfrey plantations in bounds. After flowering for a while, comfrey can start to look bedraggled but then it's time to cut it down to add to the compost. It will quickly grow a new crop of rich, attractive foliage.

Medicinal Uses

Comfrey has had a reputation as a healing herb since around 400 B.C. The Greeks used it to stop heavy bleeding, to treat bronchial problems and to mend broken bones. Herbalists today are just as enthusiastic about comfrey's healing properties which have also been confirmed by scientific research. Knitbone and boneset are alternate common names given this plant, which is effective both externally and internally for fractures, sprains, bruises and burns. (Some authorities are worried about possible liver damage from internal application but results to corroborate such a link have come from massive test-feedings to rats and horses.) It is the compound allantoin in comfrey that heals inflammation and helps to rebuild tissue by promoting cell growth. Comfrey root has strongly antiseptic tannins as well as the highest mucilage content of any herb. Thus a root decoction, made by actively boiling the root in water, is very soothing and healing for coughs, ulcers plus respiratory and bronchial ailments. Comfrey also helps the pancreas to regulate blood sugar levels.

For external use, pulp and apply fresh comfrey leaves as a poultice or alternately, soak a cloth in a heated brew of leaves or roots, wring and apply. Internally, a standard tea of one teaspoon (5 mL) of dried leaves per cup (240 mL) of liquid is not only beneficial for internal sores and inflammations but, simply as a beverage to enjoy, it is delicious and very high in chlorophyll and vitamins.

Culinary Uses

Comfrey would undoubtedly be a popular fresh vegetable if its leaves weren't covered with rough prickly hairs. To use in a salad, the leaves need to be cut fine. But steaming for a minute gets rid of the "pricklies" and what roughness remains is more than made up for in taste and richness.

Garden Uses

Comfrey has notable medicinal and edible uses but its garden uses are just as praiseworthy. It sends its roots four to eight feet (1.2 m to 2.4 m) deep into the subsoil, bringing up all sorts of nutrients and it will grow an enormous amount of leaf each year. This protein-rich (17 percent) foliage can be cut often and added to the compost pile where its low carbon to nitrogen ratio helps the rapid breakdown of other compost materials. It has more than twice the potassium of first-class manure and a little more nitrogen as well. Because of its high concentration of soluble plant food, comfrey can be made into a potent manure tea. Steep one part comfrey leaves in three parts water for a few weeks to make a crash dose of potassium and other minerals for tomatoes, root crops, cucumbers and squash. The brew can be poured on the ground beside the vegetables or sprayed on the leaves as a foliar feed. Comfrey leaves can also serve as a great mulch to put around other vegetables and herbs.

Whether comfrey and sunroot become friends or foes in your garden is largely up to you. Some may consider them noxious weeds, along with many other native wild plants. For others, like myself, their vitality and versatility make them likely candidates to help us create vibrant, self-sustaining gardens.

11

Vegetable Soup

Though I've hardly mentioned most of our common vegetables and herbs until now, it's not because I advocate replacing them with the likes of amaranth and echinacea. I love to grow whatever I can in my gardens. However, given the wealth of excellent gardening publications that are already available, I don't wish to duplicate information that represents experience far more encompassing than my own. I've been gardening for only fifteen years. Still, I can't resist passing on what are, to me, some of my most significant learnings about familiar garden crops.

I've always had the gardening urge. Even as a kid growing up in Montreal, I tried to convince my parents to convert some of our well-manicured lawn to vegetable-growing space. I was only allowed to grow carrots in a three foot square patch under our back porch. I vividly remember astonishing my aunt with evidence that carrots didn't grow

117

on trees! However, it wasn't until 1975, when I moved to Salt Spring Island off British Columbia's mainland, that I grew my first garden. As a Salt Springer, I've been gardening a green gallop ever since. The following are a collection of observations culled from my garden notebooks.

The Right Start

Most fascinating to me in my garden pogo-hopping are not only the number and diversity of ways in which gardeners grow vegetables but also that almost all of these methods work well. The number of planting methods alone is staggering. You may thin thickly or not at all. You may weed religiously or once in a while. You may plant by the moon or by the sun. But whatever the method, whatever the potting mix, no matter how you seed your rows or whether you plant in troughs or hills, there's one thing I believe crucial to vibrant vegetable culture—good soil. All our common vegetables thrive in loose, rich, moisture-retaining soil— much more so than for the plants I've already discussed. Good soil—the product of a program that incorporates composting and/or green manuring and/or mulching—is essential.

Whenever possible, I grow my vegetables and herbs in wide, deeply-dug permanent raised beds, a method that is receiving greater appreciation and is discussed in many gardening books. The soil in raised beds drains quickly and warms up early. Soil compaction is reduced because the beds aren't walked, on which allows air and water to reach plant roots more easily. Crops can be planted more intensively because of the depth to which the soil has been worked. Compost, mulch, green manures and organic fertilizers are more economical on permanent beds and don't have to be employed on unproductive garden paths.

Greens

Greens have been bred to produce thick, succulent leaves and some-times juicy, tender stalks—but only in fertile, moist soil. Outer leaves can often be harvested, allowing the centre of the plant to keep growing. Greens don't store well: they should be cooled quickly after harvest and kept in conditions of high humidity.

Brassicas

I always get best results by starting transplants of the following cabbage family members: broccoli, cauliflower, Brussels sprouts, cabbage, collards and kohlrabi. My best kale plants though, are usually volunteers. I pot up (i.e. transplant to a slightly larger container) a couple of times, each time into more fertile soil, and try to maintain uninterrupted growth. The larger the brassica before it's planted out as an offering to root maggots and cutworms, the better.

Kale and collards have the highest vitamin and mineral content of the brassicas; cousin broccoli is highly nutritious as well. Broccoli leaves and stems have a greater concentration of nutrients than the heads; I find Romanesco broccoli to be the most tasty and beautiful variety of them all. My favorite cabbages are the Savoys: they are the easiest to grow well, are higher than others in vitamin A, plus withstand and improve with frost. Brussels sprouts also taste better after frost and they are almost as winter hardy as kale; picking off their lower leaves as the plants grow tall encourages sprouting, but leave ten to twelve leaves on top.

Celery

I seed my celery early in flats and transplant it two months later when the nights start to warm. Celery grows slowly and also drinks and feeds heavily. Although it is not essential to grow it in mucky soils as some claim, it does need lots of humus that never dries out. The first time I tasted homegrown celery its full taste and lack of bitterness was a revelation that totally changed my opinion of this stalwart, otherwise pallid vegetable.

Chard

This hardy member of the beet family doesn't bolt to seed in hot weather as readily as spinach and lettuce. A copious producer, four to six plants can supply the average family with ample greens for salad and steaming. Chard keeps producing as you cut the outer leaves and will last long after fall frosts. Although the leaves do not do well over winter unless protected, the roots often survive, producing very early spring greens. A particularly beautiful variety is Rhubarb chard.

Lettuce

In my experience, almost all lettuce varieties are good if grown under proper conditions. A light and nourishing soil, cool to temperate weather and constant even moisture are keys to success. I favor Romaines—I find them to be the fastest growing, largest yielding and most flavorful of lettuces. They are also reputed to be much higher in vitamins A and C than other lettuces.

Asparagus

Freeing your bed of perennial weeds at the outset is most important for this gastronomic delight of early spring. Planting the crowns four to six inches (10-15 cm) deep rather than the recommended deeper levels results in higher yields and reduces susceptibility to root rot. Harvesting second and third year asparagus does not decrease future yields, as is commonly believed. Asparagus requires little additional fertilizer so long as your soil is fertile to begin with.

Roots

Root crops grow best in well-loosened soil that allows uninterrupted root growth. Usually slow to germinate and emerge, they should be sown in ground that is as weed-free as possible.

Beets

Some gardens routinely exhibit beautiful, luscious beets while others do not. Beets are sensitive to nutrient and trace mineral deficiencies. They do best in light, fertile, evenly moist and well-drained soil with a pH of 6.2 to 7.0. Dolomite lime and seaweed or seaweed fertilizer often give beets a considerable boost. Beet seedlings are rather weak and have difficulty penetrating crusty ground, so a surface coating of humus is most helpful.

Winterkeeper, Always Tender, Long Season and Lutz are similar beet varieties that produce large and irregular roots; they have the best edible greens and supersweet flesh that doesn't get fibrous with age. For most of North America, they can be seeded from mid-May to mid-July for fall and winter harvests. In the southern U.S., they are best sown in the fall or early spring. Cylindra and Formanova are fine varieties whose long cylindrical shape makes them easy to cut into identical round slices.

Carrots

I've always found it worthwhile to screen sticks and stones from my intended carrot bed—a time-consuming process, but it results in long, straight and even carrots. It is a lot easier to seed carrots thinly than to thin them severely. As with beets, crusting can often prevent seedling emergence: use compost or sieved soil on the surface and keep your soil fairly moist until the seedlings emerge. Water deeply so the roots go down, but avoid soaking mature carrots or they may crack. Keep carrot crowns covered or they'll turn green or purple from sunlight.

Leeks

I've never found it necessary to trench or hill leeks and I've still won the blue ribbon at our local fall fair. Leeks are a gourmet item whose price always remains high, so they make an excellent cash crop if you have space in your garden. They like a lot of organic matter in the soil but don't like competition with weeds. With heavy mulch, they'll grow year round in coastal and many inland locations. My favorite variety has one of my least favorite names—Unique Leek.

Onion

I usually seed my onions and leeks indoors in early February. Onions are high yielders and have fairly high fertility requirements. Their shallow roots need constant moisture for best growth. All members of the onion family do best in a weed-free environment. As onion bulbs grow on the ground, it's best to set plants as shallowly as possible and firm them carefully. When the bulbs begin to swell, pull the soil away to give them maximum exposure. Avoid watering onions when they reach full size.

Parsnips

This care-free vegetable is best if allowed to grow late in the fall. With exposure to cold and a few frosts, it takes on a sweet, nutty flavor and crispness. Parsnips can be left in the ground over the winter under a heavy layer of mulch but are best harvested and used quickly as soon as Spring springs: if they start growing in the ground again, they will become tough and woody.

Potatoes

Gardening manuals always say to plant potatoes in acidic soil. Most of the gardens I work and play in have close to a neutral pH but my potatoes thrive anyway. They sometimes get potato scab, which is associated with alkaline soils, but these raised scabby marks can be peeled off easily and don't affect flavor. Keep the soil around potatoes loose and free of weeds but practise shallow digging so as not to puncture tubers. Potatoes need lots of water but avoid growing them in soggy, hard-packed soil.

Potatoes yield a fivefold greater crop per unit land area than either wheat or corn. They are a good source of protein, dietary fibre, carbohydrate, vitamin C and potassium but contain practically no sodium or fat. The potato's reputation as a fattening food probably comes from the butter and sour cream that is often slathered on it: a potato contains only a few more calories than an apple. The recent introduction of many new varieties greatly extends the range of available tastes and textures. One of my family's favorites is the Canadian-introduced yellow potato, Yukon Gold. It is a high yielder, fine keeper and it has excellent taste and texture no matter how it's cooked.

Fruits

Vegetables grown for the harvest of their fruits grow best in the most fertile soil that you can provide. With the exception of peas, all are sensitive to frost and poorly adapted to cool, damp weather.

Corn
A good corn crop demands very fertile soil and lots of water. In fact, if one were totally serious about sustainable gardening, neither corn nor celery would be grown unless one had excess heaps of organic waste. Both are gluttons for nourishment and return to us relatively little of it compared to other vegetables. But what could replace the versatility of celery (try drying leaves for flavoring soups) or the taste of fresh corn on a late summer evening?!

Cucumber
Picky about proper conditions, cucumbers like heat, moisture, a well-drained, fertile soil and some shade. I like growing them in the partial shade of tomatoes in a greenhouse or in the corn patch outdoors. They need a lot of space and something to climb on. Because they grow so quickly in warm weather, I usually wait until early June to direct seed them. My family enjoys the round yellow variety called Lemon cucumber, which has the advantage of being less likely to get bitter under stress from excessive heat or irregular watering. Of all the regular slicing cukes, I've most appreciated the growing and eating qualities of the open-pollinated Marketmore varieties.

Eggplant

Definitely a greenhouse or cloche plant here on the coast, eggplant requires hot days and nights if it is to develop sizeable fruit. Though I'm not normally enthusiastic about hybrids, I have to say I grow Dusky eggplants year after year and they've never disappointed me.

Peas

I usually plant peas as early as possible so I can follow them with a winter vegetable. I find though that they do well in hot weather as long as their feet are constantly wet. Sugar Ann peas are as succulent as their towering parent Sugar Snaps but they grow low enough to support themselves if planted in blocks. I always grow a soup pea variety called Capucijners, which dries on the vine by mid-July. They cook up into a thick, rich and delicious broth that's capable of sustaining one through any winter night.

Peppers

Although peppers need full sun, I don't find them to be a hot weather crop like eggplant. Once established, moderately cool nights don't seem to set them back, but on the hottest summer days, they seem to appreciate the cooling effects of mulch. Peppers need a well-drained soil and are best watered thoroughly but not frequently. I've grown dozens of different hot peppers and the Cayennes have always been the hardiest and most prolific. I've found that by bringing pepper plants indoors over winter and keeping them relatively dry, I've been rewarded by early and massive harvests by early summer.

Tomatoes

Tomatoes are unusual in that they have a definite predilection for growing by themselves (though they do like basil) and in their own compost; they can be grown in the same place year after year. Like most of the above vegetables, tomatoes need constant, even moisture. I find generally that, once established, they do better outside than in a greenhouse as excessive greenhouse heat impedes fruit production. They certainly do like heat though, so mulch only after the soil has warmed up. I prefer paste tomatoes over other types: they are prolific and reliable producers that don't need staking and their taste is (to me) richer, less acidic and more robust. You can't beat cherry tomatoes for sweetness and the non-hybrid variety, Gardener's Delight, tops my list.

Squash and Pumpkins

Squash and pumpkins are sun lovers that like well-drained soil with good aeration and constant moisture. They are heavy feeders and stories abound about their antics on compost heaps. Careful transplanting into warm soil gives them a head start plus helps ensure adequate growth and full maturation.

Because of their high water content, they can't compete nutritionally with grains or beans on a per serving basis but nevertheless, squash and pumpkins are a good source of carbohydrates, vitamins and minerals. They flesh out soups and stews beautifully and make you feel that you've had a substantial repast. Their seeds are rich in oil and protein and, when roasted, are as delicious as they are nutritious.

Herbs

In the context of this book, I think the two most important herbs to mention are basil and French tarragon. Not only do they have wonderful culinary qualities, they also have great potential as cash crops to help defray expenses incurred outside the garden for materials inside the garden. Both basil and tarragon freeze well and make superb herb vinegars; unlike thyme and oregano, they lose a lot of their flavor when dried.

Basil

I usually grow my basil in cloches or in a greenhouse. It is a heat-loving plant that grows best in moist, very fertile soil and will keep producing lush greens when cut back regularly. It dies at the first hint of frost. I fertilize my basil every two weeks with a solution of compost tea or fish fertilizer.

French Tarragon

French tarragon is usually classified as a tender perennial but all my tarragon survived our record cold 1988-9 winter, whereas my so-called hardy Greek oregano did not. Tarragon likes well-drained, sandy earth and, like most other herbs (basil excepted), loses its essential qualities when it is grown in too rich a soil. Tarragon is easily multiplied by dividing the roots in spring.

My classification of greens, roots, fruits and herbs is a merging of vegetable features which I trust will give as little offense as a cook's choice in blending ingredients for a satisfying broth. I hope my brief comments on growing methods and varieties stimulate some new recipes for your own vegetable soups.

12

Winter Gardening

One of my greatest joys as a gardener is to harvest my own food in winter. At no time is it more evident that vegetables picked and eaten fresh from the garden have taste and vitality that far surpass any frozen, canned or otherwise processed food. Yet, even here on the coast where winters are temperate, few people keep winter gardens. While winter gardening is especially a coastal and southern celebration, continental gardeners too can grow at least a few of the most hardy winter vegetables until December. And various methods will allow gardeners throughout southern Canada and the northern U.S. to keep active gardens through to spring. While each situation is unique, this chapter, written by a gardener who has learned what works best at 49 degrees north latitude off the coast of British Columbia, gives general growing principles and suggests varieties and planting times.

Winter Garden Basics

It would probably be easier to consider extending the growing season if the beginning of summer weren't such a strange time to be thinking about mid-winter meals. Winter gardening means harvesting, but not planting, in winter. If you want to be eating fresh beets and broccoli in January, you'll need to have and plant your seeds by mid-July or earlier, depending on available sun hours. As with summer crops, some winter vegetables are harvested all at once while some can be enjoyed over a long period. Growing a successful winter garden means learning certain basic principles and discovering the right varieties to sow at the right time.

Potential vegetables that overwinter, or stay in the ground all winter, are presented at the end of this chapter. Of these, the most hardy are leeks, kale and Brussels sprouts, all of which can perform through spring for continental growers. After October, you can have any or all of these vegetables fresh from the garden yet scarcely have to think about watering or weeding. After the first frost some of these veggies become wonderfully delicious as their starches are converted to simpler sugars.

Planning

The timing involved with winter vegetables can be fairly complex. Annuals, such as spinach and Chinese mustards, have to be sown late enough in summer to not bolt, yet early enough for optimum growth. July and August can be either rainy or rainless months. In any case, these months are already full with harvest, vacations and other summer stuff, which can make it difficult to squeeze in winter garden plans, bed preparation, seed sowing, plus additional watering and weeding.

Beginning gardeners would do best to be selective and try plants that are most appealing to them.

Basic to gardening any time of the year is the importance of understanding local weather patterns. Here on Salt Spring Island, the cool, even, humid nature of our maritime climate allows vegetables in October and November to harden up for winter. About one year in seven, though, can prove to be disastrous for our winter gardens. We often have a period of several weeks when dry cold air from east of the coast mountains flows over, bringing continental weather. If it snows before prolonged freezing sets in, the ground and plants are insulated, but if not, some winter veggies can freeze. One can prepare for and prevent such a disaster by selecting an optimum site and using mulch, greenhouses, cloches and cold frames. (Cold frames and cloches are often interchangeable terms, though the latter usually refers to a less permanent glass or plastic cover for protecting outdoor plants.)

Most gardeners have little choice in their gardening sites but learn how to do best with what they have. A gentle, well-drained, south-facing slope is ideal for planting winter vegetables. If the site is protected from wind by buildings or other structures that don't block the sun, so much the better. Buildings reflect and hold heat and the south side of a house is usually the warmest spot. Terracing a slope also creates warm microclimates. Avoid low spots if possible as they collect cold air. Barriers to the free flow of air can cause air drainage problems: a tight shrub or fence downwind of your garden will trap freezing air instead of letting it pass by. A solid uphill barrier on the other hand, deflects cold air and damaging winds. Raised beds are an excellent idea, especially because they drain well—wet, cold soil suffocates plants. Cloches and cold frames help prevent soil from getting water-logged as well as prevent wind damage to which plants are quite vulnerable in winter. Cloches however, require more attention in terms of temperature: excessive daytime heat in winter cloches can cause plants to bolt to seed.

As with summer gardening, the amount of organic matter in the soil is important in winter. Good humus content aids aeration, buffers extremes of acidity and alkalinity, allows slower, longer-lasting nutrient release and keeps soil at a more even temperature. Light sandy soils warm up quickly and drain well but retain less moisture and are more affected by temperature changes. Heavy clay soils grow finer, hardier fall and winter crops but can become water-logged. After summer growth, don't fertilize with nitrogen for winter crops: it produces fast sappy growth that is not likely to stand up to first frost.

Planting

Winter crops should be spaced a little farther apart than summer ones to allow for greater root growth and better aeration. Wide row beds give higher production per unit of ground, provide a greater surface area of warmed soil and give improved drainage. As with regular gardening it is wise to rotate crops. You'll recall that this is the accepted practice of not growing the same vegetable or family member in the same place two or more years in a row. Rotation minimizes pests and disease problems and makes better use of the soil's resources. Unfortunately, year-round growing makes planning more complex and all the more necessary.

Maintenance

Cool greenhouses, cold frames and cloches are great for extending the growing season and protecting plants from wind, water and cold. They also protect against infestations of insects such as cabbage root fly maggot and carrot rust fly. The important thing to remember here is that winter veggies need lots of air and light.

Mulching is good for overwintering crops because it protects roots and stems during freezing weather, encourages biological activity and keeps soil loose for easy harvesting. It also suppresses early weed growth in February, March and April. Most mulches (sawdust being a notable exception), harbor slugs, so it's best to wait until plants are large enough to handle it before applying. When harvesting winter greens such as spinach, lettuce and corn salad, it is best to pick the outer leaves for the first few months to stimulate more core growth. Don't pick leaves when they are frozen as they will quickly rot: rather wait for them to thaw on the plant.

Apart from planting techniques, the specifics of which are usually on seed packets, three principles important to any successful garden should be kept in mind: stay attuned to the weather, use succession planting and keep good notes. For example, quick action in the event of an early freeze warning, such as throwing a large sheet of plastic over an area of winter cauliflower, could save the crop. Winter vegetables can be planted for early fall, late fall, winter and overwinter and some crops, such as lettuces, can be kept as small seedlings throughout the winter to resume growth in early spring. Noting planting dates is essential so that if timing was wrong, it can be adjusted the next year.

Varieties

Generally speaking, varieties of vegetables bred for the summer growing season are not suitable for winter gardens. They produce quickly but lack staying power. Winter varieties are not easy to find; you usually can't buy them from local seed racks. The best seed companies I've found for selection of overwintering vegetables include Abundant Life Seed Company, Stokes, William Dam and Territorial Seed Company, whose addresses are in the bibliography. As with most things, other peoples' recommendations may not work best for you, so it's important to keep experimenting. The same seed variety can change over the years too. If you enjoy the benefits of winter gardening as much as I do, it would be worth learning how to save your own seed to keep varieties adapted to your area. Besides, I have always found my own seed to have the most vigor and highest germination rates.

Brassicas

Purple Sprouting **broccoli** and White Sprouting broccoli are extremely cold-hardy varieties that must overwinter before flowering in March or April. It is helpful to side-dress them with compost in mid-February when spring growth begins. In a mild winter, many of the summer and fall varieties, especially non-hybrids such as Waltham, DeCicco, Romanesco and Italian Green Sprouting, can be grown through late fall and winter from July and early August sowings. These need protection from hard freezes. If using transplants, set them out by early September. Purple and White Sprouting broccoli are best started at the same time as winter beets—early July with maximum sun, June otherwise.

Brussels sprouts are very cold hardy, easy to grow and have lower fertility requirements than other brassicas. Catalogues list numerous dependable winter varieties which should be sown March to mid-June for harvesting from November through March. If using transplants set them out around the beginning of July. Keeping the leaves on protects the sprouts from endless winter rains. Other Brussels sprout varieties are available for earlier harvest—from late August on.

Cabbage can be a year-round vegetable by using succession plantings and seasonally appropriate varieties. The following varieties withstand rain, wind and freezes and can remain in good shape long after the winter holiday season: Mammoth Red Rock, Chieftain Savoy, January King, Langedyker Winterkeeper, Winterking and Wivoy. They are best started in June or early July.

Overwintering **cauliflowers** are not as hardy as overwintering broccoli, but with sufficient mulch and a mild winter, they can provide lots of fresh heads right through autumn, winter and early spring. In the past, I have been successful with a late July sowing of Armada, Early Purple Sicilian and English Winter (Leamington)—all overwintering cauliflowers which head up in March, April and May. They needn't tie up garden space for nine months for a one-cut harvest: transplants can be interplanted with maturing corn, then fava beans or other overwintering legumes can replace the corn after it's been harvested.

Collards are a non-heading cabbage that can provide greens well into winter. Like most brassicas, collards need fairly rich, well-limed soil. The best seeding time is mid-July and the most common variety is Vates. Most winters, you can harvest collards continuously, and in spring, the broccoli-like sprouts are tender and delicious.

The most cold-hardy **mustard green** is Green-In-Snow, which can be seeded in early September and makes abundant winter growth in cold frames. There are many other mustard varieties, for example Kyona, Komatsuma and Tai Sai that are more or less mustardy and pungent. On the coast, they are best sown in February in your first prepared bed—especially under Reemay or other cover to get them going. If the slugs don't get them, they'll spice up a salad or stir-fry around the beginning of May.

If you want to try overwintering just one vegetable, I heartily recommend **kale**. It is the easiest to grow, hardiest, most pest-resistant, delicious and nutritious! Many people along the west coast grow Russian Red kale in their gardens. After the first frost, its rich taste is enhanced by a fine sweetness. With a simple dressing it makes superb salad fare and is excellent steamed or cooked in soups, stews, stir-fries and pasta dishes. It has over ten times the vitamin and mineral content of other brassicas, such as cabbage and cauliflower. From a mid-July sowing, you can start picking individual leaves in late October. Little growth will occur during December and January but lots of leaves will develop again in February. This is the time to side-dress the plants with compost, bloodmeal or aged manure. When they flower later on, be sure to try eating the unopened flowers! Other hardy kales include Westland Winter, Siberian, Konserva and Green Curled Scotch.

Other Greens

Celery is hardy to about 18°F (-8°C), but the leaves get strong and bitter-tasting. To carry over your summer celeries, use a thick mulch or put them in cold frames, cloches or plastic sheds.

Endive, though much stronger tasting than lettuce, gets sweeter after frost and will survive most coastal winters with little protection. Cut in small pieces, endive will make any salad more zesty. It can be sown from mid-July to September. Good varieties are President, Wivol, Green Curled, Frisan and Broad-leaved Full Heart Winter.

I usually keep many **lettuce** varieties under cloches or in a green-house over winter. An early July to early August sowing will produce a good-sized lettuce by the time growth stops around the end of October. From then on, I harvest outer leaves except from smaller, later-sown plants, which will come on strong in March. I find almost all lettuce, except the iceberg varieties, to be good for overwintering. Four especially hardy winter lettuces are All Year Round, Brune d'Hiver, Winter Density and Winter Marvel.

Mâche or **corn salad** is another green whose flavor is enhanced by frost. Some people call it a gourmet salad green while others don't appreciate its unusual taste. It is very cold hardy and should be sown in early September. It overwinters in rosettes and then puts out abundant growth in spring. Its pretty blue flowers are also edible. Corn salad seeds and establishes its own patch quite readily. Popular varieties are Verte de Cambrai and Large Dutch.

Spinach can be planted from late July through mid-August. Overwintered spinach needs especially well-drained soil but is hardy otherwise. Tyee, Bloomsdale, Winter Bloomsdale, Giant Winter and Melody are all varieties that stand winter cold here.

Swiss chard should be sown during the first two weeks of July. It is moderately winter hardy and usually needs protection but will sprout again from the roots if the tops die. Fordhook Giant is the best for overwintering.

Roots

The best overwintering **beet** varieties are Lutz and Winterkeeper (occasionally called Long Season or Always Tender). Despite their large size, they remain amazingly sweet and tender all winter. They produce copious amounts of fine beet greens until hard frost. Cover the bed with mulch to prevent the roots from freezing during a severe cold snap. Optimum planting time is June if the growing site receives seven to nine hours of sun a day, early July if the beets get sun all day.

Most regular **carrot** varieties will keep in well-drained soil until they resprout in the spring. Raised beds help drainage and a thick mulch will protect carrots from freezing in severe cold. Mid-July is the optimum planting time under full-sun conditions. The following varieties have superior winterkeeping qualities but there are many others I haven't tried: Caramba, Fakkel Mix, Royal Chantenay, Flakkee and Berlicummer.

Parsnip seeds should be sown between early June and mid-July. Dig the roots anytime after the first frosts in October. With a thick mulch on well-drained soil, they will keep in the ground through winter. Parsnips were the potatoes of Europe 500 years ago. Some people still know how versatile and delectable they are. Harris Model and Hollow Crown are the most available varieties.

Rutabagas are a cross between a turnip and a cabbage. For large roots, plant seed by mid-July. Altasweet, Laurentian and Best of All are all hardy varieties.

Leeks are hardy, attractive, pest-free and delicious. Unlike most other vegetables suitable for overwintering they require an early start in February or March. It is amazing to think how large the delicate transplants will become when setting them out in April or May. They grow slowly but grow they do and when you're still digging out huge leeks in March, it's time to start seeding them again. The following varieties are all extremely hardy: Giant Carentan, Giant Musselburgh, Alaska, Unique and Durabel.

Potpourri

As you can see, many of our common vegetables can be right out there in the garden waiting for you to harvest them in the depths of winter. There are other fine possibilities to pursue. There are parsley varieties bred to stand up to cold weather. Chervil is as popular as parsley in Europe and is an excellent winter salad addition. Chives die down in October but reappear in late February. Fennel is a perennial that dies back in October and produces lots of anise-flavored foliage by early March. Garlic cloves send up shoots beginning in February. Horseradish can be dug all winter. Lovage is a perennial that appears very early and yields wonderfully flavorful greens for soup. French sorrel hangs on through the winter in protected spots and can impart its characteristic sour flavor to salads or soup. Sunroot, as already described, is a perennial species of sunflower whose tubers are best left in the ground until you're ready to steam or fry them; they taste better after a freeze and can be harvested all winter. Celeriac can be a very versatile winter root, tasting good in soups and stews or grated fresh in salads. There are turnips, watercress, winter radishes, and lots more vegetables and herbs for the winter gardener to discover.

This chapter details winter crops and strategies that I've found to be most appropriate for the region of the Pacific Northwest. Gardeners at corresponding east coast latitudes generally have to contend with somewhat colder winters. In those parts of North America where snow stays on the ground for several months, growers will best raise summer vegetable varieties suitable for canning or freezing. In the most southern U.S., winter gardening is easy: the toughest test of a gardener's skill is to grow food in the heat of the summer! Each bioregion presents unique conditions and offers unique possibilities for growth. For this west coast gardener, to be able in winter to pick fresh kale, carrots, beets and lettuce for use with simply-stored potatoes, squash, beans and quinoa is the icing on the sustainable gardening cake.

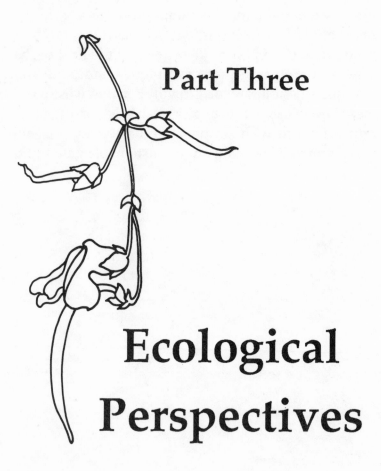

Part Three

Ecological
Perspectives

I t is one thing to grow environmentally-friendly food in an environmentally-friendly way. It is another to honor other peoples' rights to do the same. Many countries and cultures around the world had a viable agriculture until First World countries and transnational corporations began exploiting resources in the name of "development," "progress" and the "green revolution." By not examining all the costs of our food choices, we buy into such exploitation. If what we consume impoverishes other peoples' diets and destroys their environments, we must also be aware that these habits will eventually destroy our own environment.

The sad truth is that the same mentality that has laid waste Third World countries is well on its way to doing the same to North America. The monopolization of economic power with its attendant mass mechanization of resource management has almost eliminated what is needed to sustain future generations—including clean water, topsoil, diverse crop varieties and (that precious resource!) farmers.

This third section discusses the ecological ramifications of what we grow and eat; it also poses some challenges to take responsibility for our own health and well-being. Although we are entering a future that is unimaginable, we must not think that this wonderful experiment on planet Earth is doomed to failure because of a temporary sidetrack called the Industrial Age. Although we are running out of wilderness spaces and are rapidly losing species of lifeforms that reflect the immensity of our own being, we must somehow restore our faith in the intelligence of life to adapt and flourish. And we must acknowledge that what has created such great loss is an insecurity for our own existence. We think we need to control our relationship with our world as if it were alien, as if it might get us if we don't. And yet the simplicity of the smallest flower reminds us that existence is not something we have to fight for.

In the midst of the amalgamation and concentration of economic power that is a salient fact of our time, there is another movement, called bioregionalism, that is beginning to gather momentum. It has the potential to sprout seeds of change even in the midst of corporate boardrooms where such centralization is deemed profitable: multinational executives also want a green planet for their children and grandchildren. It is a movement that recognizes that we are now indeed a "global" village in certain respects, while at the same time recognizing that "villages" around the globe have their own innate integrity that should be maintained. Bioregionalists call for human society to be more closely linked to nature by becoming more conscious of the places within which they live; they believe that the areas we inhabit can nourish and sustain all our reasons for being.

In terms of growing food, the bioregional approach of local self-reliance makes infinitely more ecological sense than dependence on transportation systems and fossil fuels to move perishable goods thousands of miles across continents and around the world. To be at home in one's bioregion is to participate mindfully in its life. This includes cultivating an awareness not only of the costs of what we do but also of what we don't do. By caring for where we live, we simultaneously take care of our planet.

Greater intimacy with our natural surroundings may bring a few surprises. One of the most fascinating stories to me in my study of plants has been the original domestication of the few dozen or so food crops that have, for thousands of years, been the mainstays of the human diet. Most of the wild ancestors of these foods, which include amaranth, quinoa and the legumes discussed in the previous section, are still around, but plant researchers have been able only to speculate as to how "primitive, Stone Age" farmers brought them into cultivation. Indeed, despite incredible advances in genetics and plant breeding, modern people have domesticated few, if any, major food crops. All the important food annuals we eat today we owe largely to our nameless ancestors and to a process of creation begun long before recorded history. For me, this is evidence not only of a very ancient origin for agriculture but also of a supernal intimacy with the earth that we have long forgotten but that we can still reclaim as our birthright. Solutions to our crisis of survival on Earth exist: we must learn to find them. And who knows what aspects of ourselves may emerge to embrace us for new destinies of joy!

13

Seed Politics

A round the world a serious situation is threatening the safety of our food supply. While many people ponder the consequences of global warring and global warming, perhaps the largest environmental catastrophe is unfolding in the garden. The rapid and inexorable loss of genetic diversity in agriculture is leading us to face the possibility of worldwide hunger.

Varieties of food plants that have been grown for generations are being replaced by single, modern, scientifically spawned hybrids. Reducing the diversity of life narrows our options for an already uncertain future, when it will be essential that our food crops have resistance to pests and diseases as well as the ability to adapt to climate changes, fluctuating water supplies, ozone holes and acid rain. To simplify nature as is being done by modern agriculture is to destroy the complex interrelationships that hold the natural world together in the dramatic tension that is life. Responsibility for restoring food variety and abundance may well rest with those who love the feel of rich moist earth on their hands, and who save seed from their own home gardens.

Seed Companies

My own entry into the world of seeds was quite serendipitous. I had started growing beans, soybeans, quinoa and amaranth, naturally enough, as high-nutrient food for my family. A couple of harvests later, I found myself wanting to reveal the goodness of these crops to others. The beauty of it was, their harvests were the seeds themselves. I could give people seeds not only to cook but to plant as well. I also encouraged them to save seed from their own plantings. Little did I know that this would lead to the development of my own seed company!

Salt Spring Seeds

I was especially enthused by the Black Jet soybeans I had been successfully growing. Despite what I had read about soybeans, this variety matured in the cool summers of the Gulf Islands, was easy to digest and tasted wonderful. My enthusiasm was confirmed by many people to whom I mailed seeds across British Columbia.

I applied for aid from a government grant program to set up official test plots as a way to further legitimize the potential of Black Jets. Despite all the supporting letters I had included from gardeners who had grown them to maturity, my application was refused on the grounds that there were not enough heat units to grow soybeans in B.C. I was also told that soybeans had no economic potential as a commercial crop. Once I'd risen above my chagrin, I realized that the best way to popularize what I thought to be a valuable plant variety was to do it myself. Salt Spring Seeds was thus conceived.

As my company has grown, I've come to see that the prevalent attitude to the world of "seeds" is the opposite of my own. The contemporary approach places little or no value on the wealth of genetic material that exists on this planet. Rather, it runs parallel to our other patriarchal views that government and industry are superior to the natural order; that agrichemical companies will bring innovation and creativity to plant breeding; that our food needs can best be met by high energy-input production technologies.

The Big Players

Farmers worldwide have provided food for over 10,000 years by annually saving and selecting seed from their crops. It stands to reason that over time and in given regions, some seeds outperform others for any number of reasons. Of these, high performers of at least 50 years standing have come to be known as heirloom varieties. As the final link in this chain, these traditional, open-pollinated seeds were made available to the public through small, family owned and operated seed companies.

More recently, both government and private-sector plant breeders, basically lab scientists, have run experiments with such seeds to produce new, altered strains. Plant breeders' success in producing seed to perform under various circumstances has attracted the interest of large companies who recognize the potential profits available through seed production, patenting and distribution. As a result, huge, multinational corporations, such as Royal Dutch Shell, Sandoz and Union Carbide, have come to control and manipulate seed supplies.

The effects of these companies' involvement are far-reaching: the seed companies of yesteryear are quickly being taken over, amalgamated or replaced; public sector plant breeding is now focussed on areas of interest to the dominant corporations; as well, hardy, open-pollinated and regionally-adapted seed varieties are increasingly being replaced by hybrids, the effect of which is discussed in the next section.

Of course, where multinational giants are concerned, government soon follows. Plant-patenting legislation in Europe, for example, has already resulted in over half of all European vegetable varieties becoming extinct. In North America, nearly 4,000 commercial varieties of standard, open-pollinated vegetables are endangered because seed companies no longer carry them.

The Cost of Corporate Control

Corporate standards impose uniform agricultural strategies on diverse situations. Corporate control of agriculture alienates farmers and gardeners worldwide from traditional, sustainable food production methods and radically alters the quality of both seeds and food.

Hybrid Seeds

To understand why so many heirloom seed varieties are being dropped in favor of hybrids, some background on the terms "open-pollinated" and "hybrid" would be useful.

Open-pollinated seed produces the traits of the parent plant, or comes "true," if it has been properly pollinated. As pollination is part of nature's normal cycle, most open-pollinated seeds do indeed come true and reflect a natural stability.

Hybrid varieties result from selected mixed parentage. A simplified example would be the marriage of an early small-fruited pepper and a late large-fruited pepper to produce an early large-fruited pepper. Some hybrids never produce viable, or useable, seed. For those that do, the seed from the offspring is unreliable in that it usually reverts back to produce, in this case, either early small-fruited or late large-fruited peppers. The only way to prevent this is for breeders to take the time to stabilize the variety to consistently produce the same kind of pepper as the parent. Plant breeders did this until the 1950s. Hybridizers began to realize, however, that by not stabilizing varieties, they could realize huge profits by compelling customers to reorder seeds yearly.

The initial reaction to non-stabilized hybrids was negative. Nonetheless, massive promotional campaigns financed by corporate public relations budgets have outdone small seed companies' efforts to keep open-pollinated seeds readily available to the public. Commercial seed companies have become seed merchants rather than seed growers.

Hence, it has become increasingly difficult to get open-pollinated seeds. Those that are available come from biotechnical megafarms that could be anywhere in the world, and are not necessarily suitable for a given microclimate.

The drive to develop growers' acceptance of hybrids has been so successful that most people now assume that they are better than open-pollinated varieties. Gardeners have been converted by rows of perfectly uniform hybrid broccoli all maturing at the same time and the sweetness of hybrid corn and tomatoes. But the truth is that many open-pollinated varieties have more flavor and more flexibility than hybrids.

Open-pollinated varieties taste better because breeders can't manipulate the complex quality of flavor the way they can size or shape. One of the reasons they perform better lies in the diversity of their genetic code: open-pollinated varieties have enough of the same genes to distinguish them from other varieties, but enough different genes to produce slightly diverse characteristics. They also usually mature over a range of time. Hybrids, on the other hand, are almost genetically identical: all hybrid broccoli plants sown simultaneously will appear perfectly uniform, and will all ripen within a day or so of each other.

The diversity inherent in open-pollinated varieties allows some of them to survive even if disease strikes. In the case of hybrids, however, what destroys one plant has the potential to destroy them all. Take for example, the devastating blight of 1970 that struck and threatened to destroy the U.S. corn crop. This revealed that despite the number of brand name maize varieties available to farmers, all of these varieties, which were developed by corporate seed scientists, were genetically uniform and thus uniformly susceptible to the blight.

Hybrid seeds, whose parent lines are controlled by the corporate establishment, exist to protect corporate investment. Hybrids predominate in catalogues, they are expensive, and have little value for seed-saving purposes.

Effects on Global Agriculture

Of the top ten seed companies in the world, nine are either petrochemical companies like Monsanto or pharmaceutical companies like Ciba-Geigy. Now that such huge companies control the development, production and distribution of seeds, the high cost of this control is becoming only too evident worldwide. Plant breeders in these companies develop new varieties for purely economic reasons: uniformity, ease of transportation and shelf life. These varieties are also created to depend on high levels of fertilizers, to tolerate high levels of pesticides and to survive herbicides. The obvious reason for this is that the companies themselves manufacture these products. The results have been numerous. Qualities such as flavor and nutritional content have been sacrificed. Not only are input costs higher, but there are also greater health risks for farmers and an increased burden of toxic chemicals in our food and in our environment.

The escalation of dependency on these same transnational corporations is staggering. Farmers worldwide have been bedazzled by new hybrid wonder seeds for a few seasons, only to find that the resulting plants require increasingly greater fertilizer and pesticide inputs at correspondingly inflated prices. At the same time, heirlooms that represent hundreds and thousands of years of local adaptation have not been planted and have either been consumed or have lost their viability. Priceless genetic heritage has disappeared. As well, the soil begins to deteriorate, pests increase, yields decrease and it soon becomes apparent that the hybrids not only taste inferior but also are not suited to local growing conditions. No longer able to afford the costs associated with hybrid seeds, let alone the costs of growing their traditional crops, small-scale farmers, especially those in third world countries, bear greater and greater debt to become virtual slaves of the multinational companies.

Yes, the largest seed companies are also the largest producers of fungicides, herbicides, insecticides and chemical fertilizers. Despite the 1990s swing towards research and development of environmentally-friendly products, this is not likely to happen with seeds: there is little profit to be made in popularizing a diverse range of pest-resistant, open-pollinated crops.

Even more disturbing is the fact that technological breeding is displacing the very resource, that is the range of plant varieties, upon which the technology is based. The world food system now depends on very few plant varieties: 95 percent of human nutrition is derived from no more than 30 plants, and their genetic vulnerability is extreme. For example, two varieties of peas account for 96 percent of North American consumption of this vegetable; for dry beans, two varieties account for 60 percent and for millet only three varieties exist. Of global cereal nutrition, 75 percent is provided by three crops—wheat, rice and maize. Since 1900, over 86 percent of known apple varieties have become extinct. Since 1900, 2,300 pear varieties have become extinct.

At the rate plant varieties are currently being lost, our repasts will soon become exceedingly limited indeed.

Seeds For The Future

Many gardeners lament the loss of countless favorite varieties that were suited to the home garden but didn't measure up economically because they were irregularly-shaped, weren't the accepted color, thrived only in certain soils or couldn't stand up to shipping conditions. It also is clear that innumerable old varieties are no longer grown by families who had kept them alive for generations.

Seed Exchanges

Fortunately, many concerned growers have responded to the certainty of yet further erosion of genetic diversity by establishing thriving seed savers' exchanges. The Heritage Seed Program in Canada and The Seed Savers Exchange in the U.S., whose addresses appear in the bibliography, are inspiring projects that anyone interested in saving seeds should know about. These networks are dedicated to searching out and preserving endangered food crops as well as those varieties from older farmers that are considered heirlooms. They enable members to share wonderful and precious varieties of plants that would otherwise be unavailable. Through their publications, members learn not only about seed saving and genetic preservation but also about heritage gardens, seed companies that stock heirloom varieties and the backgrounds of cultivars which are part of our heritage. The Heritage Seed Program and The Seed Savers Exchange are addressing a very serious situation that threatens the safety of our food supply with positive action. They are living gene banks that help assure the survival of a rich agricultural and horticultural heritage for coming generations.

Growing Your Own

Growing all the seed for my seed company has opened my eyes to the perfection inherent in the genetic code of a vegetable seed. Also, I know that this perfection is only realized through the seed's interaction with all the aspects of a particular environment—of which the gardener is a major element. The seeds from plants I have grown over the longest time have the greatest vitality and vibrancy—a power that I believe has come from our mutual adaptation as they become part of a unique microclimate under my guardianship. Plants from seed I send out across the continent may be robust, but I know they can become more so when gardeners enter into an enduring relationship with them that allows their growing to be co-creative.

Saving our own seed restores agricultural creativity and genius to what it was until recent times. Saving seed fosters sustainability by fulfilling a basic need at home, instead of relying on seed companies or governments.

To my mind, the concept of patenting and "owning" a seed represents an extreme example of human entrenchment in maintaining power over others and power over nature. To say that everything in the world is private property, waiting to be discovered and possessed, sadly reflects our alienation from the natural world. The pervasiveness of such a myopic outlook places the onus on home garden seed savers to rediscover, preserve and popularize the superb food varieties that still exist, albeit tenuously, as everyone's heritage.

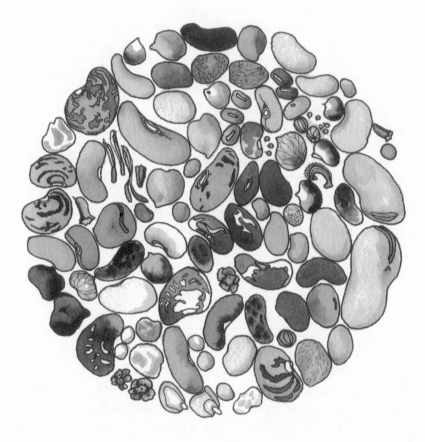

14

Saving Seed

It is hard to imagine anything more imbued with the essence of life's mystery than the very seeds with which we plant our gardens. What in life more fully symbolizes the cycle of life, death and renewal than the seed of life itself? Yet, as we've seen in the last chapter, the very existence of many seeds is threatened by corporate and government intervention and control over them. As disheartening as this situation is, we as individuals retain the freedom to choose how we will respond.

It seems timely to begin the gradual process of return toward more sane and practical attitudes that honor, rather than diminish seeds, the life-giving channels on which our existence depends. Saving seeds to perpetuate our gardens requires little financial outlay and minimal effort. This chapter outlines what you should know to begin this process.

Background Information

Because plants in nature produce seeds so efficiently without a gardener's help, to save seeds, we merely allow the selected plant to follow its natural life cycle. Only in certain instances is it necessary to facilitate this process as, for example, when vegetables are grown in climates that prevent their maturation, or for crops whose refined characteristics demand some assistance. Head lettuce and cabbage, for instance, are two vegetables that need some help in releasing their seed stalks.

Saving seed needn't be a yearly task, as most seeds that are properly stored will last from three to five years. With cooperation among several gardeners, each may save seed from a few plants to exchange with others. No special tools or machines are needed to plant, cultivate and bring crops to maturity for seed. Simple tools that facilitate the processing of seed are discussed later. Labelling plants and keeping records of planting, flowering and maturation dates as well as observations on disease resistance, yield and other special characteristics are invaluable and will ease the process in subsequent years. Generally, though, seed saving is a simple procedure which brings satisfaction from knowing that you'll enjoy repeat performances from your favorite plants.

Plant Types

Despite its ease, seed saving requires some understanding of basic plant science: the distinction between annual, perennial and biennial plants, and between self-pollinated and cross-pollinated crops. Annual plants flower and mature seed in the same year. Perennials live and bear seed year after year, which means you never have to save their seeds—unless of course you wish to expand your crop. Biennial plants are normally harvested in their first summer or fall but do not produce seed until winter has passed. Therefore, to ensure that seed will be produced to create a new crop in year three, you can assist plants in successfully overwintering. In mild coastal or southern areas, biennials will survive the winter under a cover of mulch. In most of continental North America, biennials must be dug up and carefully stored elsewhere during the winter to be replanted in the spring. Most biennials become tall and bushy when going to seed, taking up more space than they did the previous year. They should therefore be thinned or transplanted to twice the usual spacing.

Common Vegetable Types

Annuals	*Perennials*	*Biennials*
Beans	Asparagus	Beets
Broccoli	Horseradish	Broccoli
Chinese Cabbage	Rhubarb	Brussels Sprouts
Corn		Cabbage
Cucumber		Carrot
Eggplant		Cauliflower
Lettuce		Celeriac
Pea		Celery
Pepper		Onion
Pumpkin		Parsley
Spinach		Parsnip
Squash		Swiss Chard
Tomato		Turnip

Self- vs. Cross-Pollination

Pollination is the process by which pollen grains are carried from one plant part to another. In self-pollinated plants, this process occurs within each flower, with no pollen being transferred from one flower to another, either on the same plant or between plants. Such flowers have both male and female plant parts and have the mechanism necessary for pollination to occur successfully within the single bloom. Self-pollinated vegetables such as beans, peas, lettuce, peppers, eggplant, tomatoes, endive and soybeans also are, or act as, annuals, which makes them easiest to work with if you're just beginning to save seeds. The seeds of these plants almost always retain the quality of the parent seed, or stay "true." Because they rarely cross with another variety of the same species, isolating them is unnecessary unless absolute purity in a strain is desired.

Most other familiar vegetables, such as corn, carrots, beets and broccoli, are cross-pollinated—the pollen from one flower fertilizes another flower, either on the same or another plant. The pollen is carried by either wind or insects. It is important to know the other varieties of the same species with which a plant has the potential to exchange pollen. Factors specific to various plants are given later, but allowing only one variety of each potentially cross-pollinating vegetable to flower out eliminates the need to separate plants from each other.

Seed Selection

Nature has a definite role to play in terms of which vegetables you'll select for seed-saving purposes: you can't save seed from plants that don't mature. On the other hand, the gardener has a number of selection criteria. In practice, many gardeners simply want to preserve their longtime favorite vegetables. But others may wish to select for specific criteria—a subjective matter since nearly everyone has a different concept of what is ideal. No matter what combination of characteristics you're looking for, always consider the whole plant.

Criteria

Depending on your needs and preferences, criteria for selection may include any of the following: flavor, size, disease-, drought- and/or insect-resistance, lateness to bolt, trueness to type, color, shape, thickness of flesh, hardiness or storability. As an example, the northern gardener might select for earliness: this may mean tagging your earliest bean or tomato plant for seeds when you'd love to be savoring its taste. (Not that it can't be sampled, but of course the more you leave, the more seeds you'll save!) Similarly, the southern seed saver is more likely to allow luscious lettuces to grow unharvested to select for bolt-resistance in hot weather.

General Tips

For cross-pollinated plants, it is important to maintain vigor by saving seed from at least several individual plants of the same variety, even if you only need a few seeds. In any planting, cross-pollinated vegetables may look identical but some will be genetically different. Saving seed from only one or two plants, known as inbreeding, severely reduces necessary genetic contributions and results in reduced vigor and yield in succeeding generations. (Exceptions to this rule are squashes and pumpkins which do not noticeably lose vigor even if inbred for several generations.) Roguing is the term for discarding undesirable plants. For cross-pollinated crops, this must be done before plants flower.

Self-pollinated plants, such as beans and tomatoes, inbreed automatically, so you can use as many plants as you wish for seed purposes. Seed from exceptional single plants, however, could be saved separately to increase the chance of retaining its special characteristics.

Hybrid seed, as discussed in the previous chapter, results from crossing two parent plants that are genetically different. Hybrid vegetables will usually be more vigorous and uniform than either of the parents or similar open-pollinated varieties for one season. Seed from hybrid plants, however, will either be sterile or begin reverting back to the parent varieties, so is generally not worth saving.

Harvesting and Storage

The period of time available to harvest the seed of any one crop usually extends over two or three weeks because most plants don't ripen all their seed at the same time. When over half the seeds are dry, cut down entire stalks or seed heads and let them further dry indoors or in the sun, depending on the weather. Alternately, gather the seed over several weeks by bending stalks into paper bags and stripping or shaking the ripe seeds loose. If bad weather threatens at the end of the season, seeds that are almost mature can be brought indoors for further drying.

Tools

Some simple tools will make processing seed easier. A fan or hair dryer can be used to separate the good, heavy seeds from hollow seeds and other light material, such as leaves and pods. Winnowing, or tossing seed above a container, does the same thing: light material is carried away by the wind. Screens of various meshes, with or without frames, are also handy. They'll help you separate good seed from other material of similar weight, but different size, such as pebbles, soil, twigs and seed of other crops.

Drying

Seeds should be as dry as possible before they are stored. It is a good rule of thumb to let harvested seed dry for at least a few days after being removed from the plant. The larger the seed, the longer the drying period required. Most seeds will dry adequately for home storage if spread on paper towels, newspapers or screens in an airy place for a week. They should be turned and spread several times during that period and the paper should be changed if wet. An equally good drying method is to let the seed heads or stalks dry in open paper bags for one or two weeks. The drying process can be hastened by spreading the seed in a sun-exposed room, a non-humid greenhouse or in the sun outside if it is covered or brought in at night. Lacking sun and/or greenhouse, drying can be speeded up by gentle heat as long as the temperature never rises above 100°F (38°C).

Storing

Seed should always be stored under cool, dry conditions. Temperatures well below freezing will not harm seeds unless their moisture content is high. Viability is increased by sealing most seeds from air, except in the case of beans and peas, which like some "open air." Most sound vegetable seeds, if stored properly, will remain viable for many years, with the exception of short-lived onion, leek, corn and parsnip seed. Put each kind of seed into its own envelope with the cultivar name and the date of storage. You can also put envelopes in airtight tins or glass jars with snap or rubber gasket lids that can be tightened to make them moisture proof. Longevity can be increased by storing seed jars or tins in the freezer.

Plant Specifics

While I've referred primarily to vegetables, should you wish to save seed for beans, quinoa, amaranth or soybeans, consult the appropriate chapters. I've yet to see any crosses in the beans despite having grown different varieties quite close together. As for amaranth and quinoa, I sometimes deliberately allow varieties to cross-pollinate and select from the most robust plants.

Following are brief instructions for saving seed of some of the most common vegetables. For greater detail or if you are seriously interested in preserving genetic varieties, consult the appropriate sources in the bibliography.

Biennial Root Crops

These vegetables produce their edible crop the first season and their flowers and seeds the second season. As they need overwintering to complete their cycle, they can be left in the ground or brought indoors, depending on location and preference. Anywhere you can grow them as a winter crop, it is of course practical to let some choice plants ripen seed.

Plant seed of biennial root crops early enough so that the plants will be mature at the end of the growing season. When digging up plants for storage, choose healthy plants that show characteristics desirable to the variety. Don't save seed from plants that bolt to seed the first season.

It is beneficial to prepare roots for storage by curing. This is a process which dries and toughens the skin but still leaves the root firm and plump. Curing enables the root to resist moulding and heals small breaks in the skin which would otherwise invite decay. Harvest the roots on a dry day, when the soil isn't too wet. Gently shake or rub off any excess earth. Cut the tops off about an inch above the crown and then lay them to dry, either in the sun for a few hours or indoors for a day or so. Turn them once so that all parts are exposed to air.

Beets are cross-pollinated by the wind. The pollen is very light and can be carried long distances so it is best to raise seed of only one variety each year. If you bring your beets indoors, pull them in the fall before heavy frosts. Half a dozen beets is adequate for most needs. Cut their tops an inch above the crown. Handle beets carefully as damaged ones may rot. Your storage system should provide even moisture to prevent the beets from shrivelling. A storage temperature of 40 to 50°F (4 to 10°C) favors subsequent seed stalk production more than a temperature closer to freezing. Layering beets in a box between dampened sand or fresh sawdust is a good storage method. If left in the ground, beets don't need their tops cut off but they should be protected from frost.

In the second year, beets should be thinned or replanted to about two feet (60 cm) apart, the crowns even with the soil surface. When, in the summer, most of the seeds have the brown color that indicates maturity, cut entire plants at ground level and hang them upside down in a dry, protected area. As many gardeners know, beet seeds are actually seedballs, each containing up to six seeds. When plants are completely dry, seed balls are easily stripped by hand from the branches. An alternate harvesting method is to bend each seed stalk over into a large bag and strip off the mature seeds, repeating the process when more seeds are mature.

Beets and **Swiss chard** will cross with each other, so avoid saving seeds from both crops in the same season. (Which of course doesn't prevent you from growing both for food.) Swiss chard is extremely hardy and, for seed saving purposes, there is usually no need to dig up and store the plants.

Carrots are cross-pollinated by a variety of insects. They will cross readily with Queen Anne's Lace, so it's important to keep this wild plant clipped so as not to flower at the same time as your carrots. Carrots and parsnips do not cross.

Carrots can be harvested in the fall before the ground freezes, selected for desirable appearance and stored at high humidity and near-freezing temperatures. They can be kept in boxes of damp sand or sawdust. To select for taste, cut off the crown, or top inch of the root for replanting; the rest of the carrot can then be eaten. (This can also be done for other root crops, such as beets and parsnips.) In the spring, replant tops or whole carrots a foot (30 cm) apart. Carrots will often survive outside under heavy snow cover. In mild areas they can be left in the ground under thick mulch.

Carrots grow up to six feet (1.8 m) high the second year. Each has a large head with a series of branches beneath it. The flower heads are given the name "umbel" to describe flower-clusters in which stalks nearly equal in length spring from a common center. Seed umbels mature unevenly; it's best to harvest when secondary heads have ripe brown seed and third-order heads are starting to turn brown. This is usually around September of the second year. Heads can be removed as they mature or entire plants can be pulled, formed into small piles and cured for a few weeks until the stalks will snap when bent.

Leeks are pollinated by honey bees. They may cross with onions. Generally they overwinter easily. Early tall-stemmed summer types should be hilled up with soil or mulched heavily. Rogue out and eat the less desirable plants in the fall. The second year individual plants will send up single stalks four-feet to five-feet (1.2-1.5-m) high capped by beautiful, huge umbels composed of hundreds of flowers. Pick these flower heads in the fall and dry them well. Brisk rubbing will extract the seeds.

Onions are pollinated by honeybees and they will probably cross with leeks. Harvest them as normal in fall and rogue out double onions and those with thick necks. As onions are not heavy seed producers, choose 15 to 18 of your best bulbs. Larger bulbs will produce more seed. Prepare your onions for storage by curing them as you do for your eating onions. Check that the neck area, where the tops join the bulb, is shrivelled and well dried. The best storage conditions are dry, airy and cool. Be careful not to bruise or injure the bulbs and replant them as early in spring as possible. In mild areas and especially with sweet onions that don't store well, it is better to leave the plants in the soil over winter. Cover the bulb, leaving its top barely exposed. Large flower heads above three-foot to four-foot (0.9 to 1.2m) stalks develop over several weeks in summer. Start harvesting when the fruits open to expose the black seed. Cut off the umbels as they become ready and dry them in trays, bags, on screen or canvas, in sun or under cover, stirring them occasionally. Seed should dry to the point where it is easily rubbed from the heads. Drying will often take over two weeks. Seed life is only a year or two.

Parsnips are hardy cross-pollinated biennials that are usually planted in the spring in cold climates and in mid-summer in mild areas. As with carrots, you can choose to plant only the crowns. The mature seed is dry and light brown by the next summer and shatters, or falls off the plant readily, so harvest should not be delayed. Parsnips don't cross with carrots.

Cross-pollinated Annuals

Broccoli is most often treated as an annual but overwintering varieties can be allowed to flower and set seed the following spring and summer. For regular broccoli, an early spring sowing is recommended for seed-saving since flowering is most strongly induced by the long days of early summer. Broccoli is normally cross-pollinated by bees, so it is best to grow only one variety or isolate two or more varieties considerably. Broccoli will cross with cabbage, Brussels sprouts, cauliflower, collards, kale and kohlrabi, so must not be flowering at the same time as any of these. As for other brassicas, broccoli seed is borne in narrow pods. Harvest when pods are dry and brittle. Plant stalks can be laid on tarps or canvas for further curing outside or branches of pods can be placed in open paper bags and dried in the sun. Threshing can be done by hand, flailing or by rubbing the seedpods gently through screen.

Corn is cross-pollinated by the wind so isolation is essential. Any one corn (sweet, ornamental, dent, flint, flour or pop corn) will cross very easily with any other and a neighbor's corn should be at least a quarter mile away. Late and early varieties can be planted beside each other if the first variety sheds its pollen before the silks appear on the second. Harvest when cobs are dry and give them additional drying under cover. Husks of six to eight ears can be tied together and hung in an airy place. When seeds are sufficiently dry, it is usually easy to hold an ear in one hand and twist off the kernels in another. The kernels can also be left on the cobs to be displayed through the winter. Storage life is only a year or two.

Cucumbers are pollinated mainly by bees and don't cross with other vine crops. Let the fruits ripen past the edible stage, when they will become golden, yellow or white. It doesn't matter if the vines are killed by frost. Slice the fruits in half lengthwise and scoop the pulp and seeds into a non-metallic container. Leave the mixture in a warm place and stir it a few times daily. Fermentation will reduce the jelly-like pulp around each seed to a thin liquid and will be complete in three or four days. The best seeds will sink to the bottom of the container and the lighter, inferior ones will rise to the top. Pour off the floating seeds, wash those remaining by stirring them in a few changes of water or washing them in a sieve, and then spread them on paper or screens. Dry them outdoors in sunny weather or in a warm airy room, stirring periodically to encourage uniform drying, until they feel rough but not slippery to the touch.

Squash and **pumpkins** are also pollinated by bees. The four different species of squash and pumpkins won't cross with cucumbers and melons. They will cross with their own species members, however. (Consult the seed savers' literature or grow only one variety of a known favorite for starters.) Summer squash must be left on the vine past its normal harvesting date until the skin becomes as hard as that of winter squash. All squash and pumpkins may be left past the first fall frost. Cut the fruit of the mature pumpkin or squash in half. Remove the seeds and moist material around them with a large spoon, place it all in a large bowl, add some water and work the mixture through the fingers. The seeds will separate gradually. Wash them again and spread them out on paper or screens to dry for a week or more, moving them about daily so they don't remain in small wet piles. If kept in a sealed jar, check them after a few weeks to see if there is any sign of moisture. If so, take them out for additional drying.

Spinach has a very fine pollen which can be carried a mile or more by the wind. Rogue or remove plants that bolt to seed first. Spinach seed normally ripens unevenly in the latter part of summer. Strip mature seeds from the stalks with your hands.

Biennial Brassicas

Brussels sprouts, cabbage, collards, cauliflower, kale and **kohlrabi** are all members of the cabbage family that, like broccoli, are pollinated mainly by bees, and require isolation from each other and other varieties of themselves for true seed. Unlike broccoli, they are biennials so must be overwintered outside or taken into storage conditions of high humidity and near-freezing temperatures. If replanting in spring, set plants two to three feet apart. For cabbages, it is common practice to make cross cuts about an inch (2.5 cm) deep into the top center of each head to facilitate emergence of the seed stalk. Staking keeps cabbages, which grow to five feet (1.5 m) the second year, from falling over. Cauliflower is the most difficult of the cabbage family to raise for seed in cold climates because most varieties do not overwinter well either by indoor storage or by thick mulching outdoors. Pods of all the brassicas burst open as they become dry and brittle, so harvesting them a little early and curing them further in paper bags after harvest is a good way to avoid losing any seed. Storage life of brassica seed is about five years.

Self-pollinating Annuals

Eggplants should be allowed to mature on the plant past the edible stage. The seed of one fruit is enough for several hundred plants. Cut the fruit in half, scoop out the seeds and wash them free from pulp by stirring them in water. They will separate and sink to the bottom. Don't ferment them but dry them immediately in thin layers on paper or screen. If after drying they are stuck together, rub them gently to separate them. Seeds remain viable for only a year or two.

Lettuces seldom cross but don't allow undomesticated varieties, such as Wild or Prickly Lettuce, to flower nearby. Some varieties require early spring planting to complete the seed-maturing process. In mild areas, fall-sown plants will usually overwinter, while for heading varieties, such as Iceberg and Great Lakes, it is advisable to peel back the head leaves to expose the growing point as soon as the heads mature. After the yellow flowers have their show, they start to get a feathered appearance as they go to seed. The seed will mature unevenly. Gather it every few days by bending the stalks into a paper bag and gently tapping or shaking the ripe seeds off. Late bolting is an important characteristic to select for in lettuce.

Peas will mature seed in mid-summer from an early spring planting. The seeds will rattle in their pods. Thresh them by hand and further dry them until they can't be dented with your fingernail.

Peppers are treated as self-pollinating annuals although they are perennials in warm climates. Most bell peppers ripen a rich red. A few fruit will supply seed for hundreds of plants. Remove the seed mass, allow it to air dry and rub it to separate the seed. Alternately, wash the seed with water in an appropriate container; the debris will float and the seeds can be immediately dried by spreading them out in the sun or in a warm place indoors.

Tomatoes should be selected from the best ripe plants. Scoop the seed and pulp into a suitable container and stir the mixture a few times a day. Three days of warm fermentation will reduce the pulp surrounding each seed to a thin liquid, and the sound seed will sink to the bottom of the container. The fermentation also helps destroy spores of disease organisms that may be lying dormant on the seed coat. When the seed has settled, add water, stir, and allow the seed to settle again. Pour off the liquid and repeat the process a few times. Pour the seeds into a sieve, remove any remaining bits of tomato and shake off any excess water. Dry the seed on fine meshed screen or on waxed paper in the sun or in a warm airy place. Tomato seed dries within a day in sunny weather. Seed that is stuck together can be rubbed between the hands.

Vegetative Reproduction

Potato plants sometimes produce seeds but they normally are of no use to the seed saver since they will not produce true. Crossings don't occur. Choose only healthy plants for reproduction because it is particularly easy for diseases to be passed on from one generation to the next. A few hours of drying outside toughens the skins for storage. How well potatoes keep doesn't seem to be affected by washing or not washing them. Burying them in dry sand is an excellent storage method. They should be kept in the dark.

In Summary

As the above descriptions hopefully show, seed saving procedures are quite easy once basic principles are grasped. I have omitted what is the most enjoyable technique for many seed savers—pollination by hand when cross-pollinating varieties are flowering near each other. This subject, as well as more sophisticated seed saving methods, is covered at length in the publications of the major North American seed exchanges mentioned in the previous chapter and listed in the bibliography.

Growing plants from one's own seed bestows a special and unique feeling: it has a rightness that no doubt comes from the fact that human existence on this planet has for ages been so linked to that very activity.

15

Food Choices For Sustainability

"There's only one thing that money can't buy and that's true love and homegrown tomatoes." (Well-known folk song.)

Living in the country, I know what meat from free-range animals looks and tastes like, and I can appreciate a truly farm-fresh egg. A tomato purchased at the supermarket may look good but we all know it won't compare to our homegrown tomato fresh off the vine. I attest that the same holds true for chili made with our own beans, garlic and peppers, or kale, picked fresh from the garden in the middle of winter.

The bulk of this book is about healthful, nourishing foods that we can grow in our backyards in ways that are ecologically sound. Growing organic vegetables, herbs, grains and legumes may seem like a minor step to you, in terms of helping the planet. But it really represents a big step forward. . .

Most of us are now painfully aware that industry and technological development have contributed greatly to our current ecological crisis. In North America, extremely sophisticated technology and centralized management combine to produce, process, promote and distribute our food and drugs. Even though many of the companies controlling this are now sincerely attempting to address environmental concerns, their primary aim is still to make a profit.

I believe that our wealth is infinite and that there will always be profits to make whereby everyone wins. But I also believe that we should decrease our reliance on the systems that have helped create our planetary crisis. This chapter outlines my personal views on why growing our own food and medicine, or making wise choices in buying them, can make a difference.

Food for Health

The current proliferation of books and magazines on health and healing seems to indicate a rapidly increasing awareness of the links between food and health.

Concerns about cholesterol and saturated fat intake, for example, are at an all-time high. We are learning that both of these factors, found primarily in meat and dairy products, raise the level of cholesterol in the blood, cause obesity, produce hardening of the arteries, and lead directly to heart disease and strokes. Overwhelming evidence points to the fact that no risk factor for cancer is more significant than diet. And study after study shows that excessive protein consumption increases the risk of diabetes, arthritis, kidney deterioration, multiple sclerosis, ulcers, chronic constipation, osteoporosis and hypoglycemia.

Yet can we live with less meat, eggs, milk, cheese, butter and yogurt? The meat and dairy lobbies run massive marketing campaigns informing us of the importance of their products. And most of the medical opinions I hear or read maintain that meat and dairy food are crucial for good health. (When I was considering becoming a doctor, however, I found that none of the medical schools to which I applied offered courses in nutrition.)

We're living in a culture that generally discourages us from taking responsibility for our own health. When we suffer from common ailments such as headache, heartburn or bloating, we tend to ask, "How can I get rid of this?" Most opt for the fast, easy way—synthetic drugs. Many people are becoming aware, however, that such symptoms may be warnings of a deeper problem and ask instead, "What is the cause of this discomfort and what can I do to prevent it from recurring or building into something larger?" I'd like to relate a personal story along these lines—something that changed my attitude to food and health forever.

Allergy Blues

As a child growing up in Montreal, Quebec, I was constantly plagued by sinus congestion. The beginning of each school year, when I tried to tell my new teachers that my name was Danny, but couldn't pronounce the "n's," was always traumatic for me. I hardly ever breathed through my nose. In those days it never occurred to anyone that diet could have anything to do with my congested condition. On my doctor's advice, I was constantly trying nasal sprays and getting allergy shots. It wasn't until I was twenty, when I lowered my consumption of milk, cheese, butter and meat, that I realized the cause of my problem: the meat and dairy products I had been devouring for years were stuffing me up. Without them, I could breathe!

Since then, I've been fascinated by the food habits of different cultures and by the relationship of nutrition to health. I'm convinced that our choice of food and its quality are of the utmost importance to our well-being.

Poisons Within

We are learning that meat and dairy consumption can overload our bodies and threaten our health. The cosmetic appearance of supermarket produce helps disguise the fact that these products pollute our bodies as well.

The huge factory farms that raise animals for milk, cheese, butter, eggs and meat are exceedingly overcrowded and unsanitary. Animals are stuffed in stalls and cages by the tens and hundreds of thousands and driven literally crazy by deprivation, disease and mutilation. To prevent loss of stock and ultimate profit, these farms are routinely doused with highly toxic chemicals to kill the parasites that breed in such conditions. Bacterial infections, such as salmonellosis, are rampant, and the indiscriminate use of antibiotics creates disease-causing agents that are invulnerable to modern drugs.

Recent studies indicate that 94 to 99 percent of the toxic biocides in our diet come from meat, fish and dairy products. (These statistics, as well as others quoted in this chapter, were obtained from *Diet for a New America* by John Robbins.) These foods end up on our plates replete also with growth and appetite stimulants, tranquilizers and steroid hormones. These are shocking facts; a powerful meat and dairy lobby plus our own disconnection from what we eat has kept them from being widely acknowledged until recently. Packaged meat and dairy foods may appear sanitary but, in reality, eating high on the food chain exposes our bodies to unprecedented combinations of chemicals and poisons.

Foods and Moods

While not yet wholly embraced by practitioners, medical research has shown that our food and/or our environment can influence mental or emotional reactions. This seems quite obvious to me. Like most people I know, I'm weakened by improper or inadequate nutrition, lack of sleep, allergies, infections, drug use and general stress. Nor do I see why it would be any different for animals. I would go further than most people and say that there are profound consequences to our health when we eat food from animals kept and slaughtered in states of fear, anger and panic. Although these effects are more subtle than overdoses of protein or poisons, I believe that they're well worth considering. I can't imagine how such a disharmonious, uncompassionate relationship with beings who share our planet can possibly nurture us.

Further Facets

Although I now rarely eat meat or dairy food, I am not suggesting that everyone follow my example, for diet is influenced by a host of complex and personal factors. I wish only to underline the need to expand our food choices, for it is the scale of North American meat and dairy consumption that seems suicidal. Studies discredit the common prejudice that meat gives strength and stamina: many of the world's most acclaimed athletes are vegetarians. Our protein needs have been grossly exaggerated. Besides, even without meat and dairy products, it's easy to get protein with our ordinary grains, nuts, legumes and vegetables, not to mention the likes of quinoa, amaranth and soybeans.

Finding vital, health-enhancing foods is no problem for those of us who grow or raise our own food. And, as consumer awareness grows, more commercial outlets will sell organic food. However, environment-sensitive food production methods presently account for only a few percent of total production and most of that consists of fruit and vegetables. It is almost impossible to find meat or dairy products that are produced according to organic standards. And while most of the people on the planet survive without animal-derived foods, we North Americans have an uncompromising addiction to them. It may be time, however, to begin questioning this practice.

In our capitalist culture, money will likely continue to dominate our thinking, but this may ultimately create a turning point in our views towards health as well. As the cost of medical care continues to escalate, perhaps we'll begin to listen to our bodies and manage our diets more effectively. Using food to stay well is undoubtedly cheaper, safer and more effective than the use of invasive techniques and synthetic drugs.

Health for the Planet

Unfortunately we can't go back to the meat and dairy farms of decades ago, except on a limited basis. We are too many people with too few resources. This brings me to some of the ecological concerns that our meat and dairy addictions raise.

We simply don't have enough land or water to maintain our current level of reliance on these products, even if we discount the alarming rate at which our population is growing. Consider the following statistics: an acre of land can produce about 165 pounds of beef, whereas the same acre could produce 2000 pounds of soybeans; the production of one pound of beef requires 2500 gallons of water, compared to 25 gallons for the same amount of quinoa. As of 1974, the livestock population of the U.S. was consuming enough grain and soybeans to feed the global population five times over.

Not only is there not enough land or water to maintain our diets of meat and dairy products, but many of the megafarms that produce them destroy what land and water is left and pollute the atmosphere as well.

Bitter Facts

It is estimated that a small-scale, hundred-head dairy operation generates as much pollution as a town with 2000 citizens.

It is estimated that 85 percent of topsoil loss in North America is directly associated with raising livestock. Seven out of eight acres of forest that are destroyed on this continent are used to graze livestock and/or grow livestock feed.

Half of all the water consumed in North America goes to irrigate land that supports feed and fodder for livestock. And that doesn't include the enormous amounts used to wash animal excrement away—water that returns to and contaminates our water supply.

And the air? On a worldwide basis, cows annually add more than 50 million tons of methane into the atmosphere and constitute one of the largest contributors to the greenhouse effect.

Some analysts have lately made a strong case for the livestock industry being the single most important factor in the destruction of the environment in North America.

Hidden Costs

I think that examining the hidden costs of all our food choices—not just our veal cutlets or frozen yogurt—is a crucial first step in moving towards a sustainable world. Consider, for example, how many trees are mowed down in tropical rainforests to create one fast-food hamburger. The answer is 68 square feet or 6 square meters. Consider also what is the point of banning lethal pesticides and herbicides in North America while continuing to produce and sell them to other countries. They come right back to us in our imported avocadoes, bananas, tomatoes, melons, coffee and chocolate. The process by which once self-supporting nations have become impoverished and denuded in order to feed our coffee, banana, meat and sugar addictions threatens the well-being of every global citizen. And what of the non-renewable resources that are squandered to bring food to us across great distances?

For example, I've come to appreciate the taste and stimulation of burdock-dandelion tea over that of coffee. I'm even more grateful for the easy availability of these native plants knowing that coffee is usually grown with poisons whose use is illegal in my own garden. Learning that the cost of meat on my plate may mean the annihilation of tropical rain forests or the pollution of North American rivers and lakes, I'm happy to grow more beans. As I become more conscious of what I consume, I feel increasingly that by taking greater responsibility for my own sustenance, I can better assist others in sustaining themselves. The sustainable gardener in me asks the organic gardener, "What more can I do to avoid relying on and drawing from someone else's garden?" This book is a catalogue of some of the possibilities I've found already.

I don't suggest we totally renounce coffee or bananas, meat, eggs or milk and I have to admit that I have not yet done so. However, we must become aware that when we buy products grown thousands of miles away and with the use petrochemical fertilizers and biocides, we choose and show approval of the following: agribusiness and monoculture; the use of non-renewable natural resources; depletion of soil fertility; erosion; displacement of small-scale and family farms; the destruction of wildlife habitats and essential tropical rainforests; increasing chronic and severe health problems of people working with these chemicals and eating foods grown and treated with them; and increasing health and environmental problems resulting from agricultural chemical run-off into ground waters.

When we buy local, organically-grown food or eat our own, we are endorsing: high quality nutrition; food security; soil-saving and enrichment techniques; energy efficiency and fewer trucks on the highways; stronger, more stable local economies; and the preservation of a sustainable environment for all Earth's inhabitants.

Our dietary choices feed into an international market that is fuelled by economics. By becoming more conscious of what we grow and consume, we take greater responsibility for ourselves and our families. We can begin by learning to discriminate between our real needs and our desires. We can attune to ways of producing and sharing food locally and we can foster trade based on reciprocity, mutual benefit and cooperation. We can respect the rights of others to exist healthfully within their own habitats. By taking food growing more completely into our own hands, we millions of gardeners across North America can effect a most radical change and lead the way to restoring natural balance on Earth. Tuning into the inherent sustainability of our immediate ecosystem fosters the ultimate sustainability of our planet. Indeed, the best place to begin is at home.

16

Co-Creating The Garden

Choices for a sustainable lifestyle are open to each individual. But the concept of sustainability embraces more than individualized response. The notion of taking care of ourselves needs to be wedded to one of being cared for. If we are to keep our planet green, we must join the circle to maintain its integrity, we must reach out to participate in its wholeness. Hands to hold are everywhere around us and, as the saying goes,"Many hands make light work."

This chapter is about levels of participation that are available for our growing. Whether our focus is personal or transpersonal, social or political, regional, national or cultural, we can make a difference by acting on the realization that we are all in this together. Who "we" are is less important than the fact that "we" together are indivisible.

Faith in Nature

We all have special experiences when a sense of unity and joy makes us forget daily concerns—a magical moment in a forest, a silencing sunset, a plunge in the ocean. There comes a profound, often unspeakable knowing that we are inseparable from what we perceive, part of a total balance that is somehow perfect. Despite such revelations, it seems inevitable that we return to striving for some imagined perfection and once again set ourselves apart from nature to achieve it.

We gardeners are luckier than most people, our gardens being a continual and multifaceted source of natural inspiration. Each garden dynamic is ever-changing and demands an openness to being in the moment. We like to think we're in charge of garden events but, when graced with those states of "at-one-ment," we're reminded that there are many things we don't control. In truth, gardeners can influence growing conditions in myriad ways, but it is not the gardener who grows the plant. The plant grows itself.

Gardeners who are open to recognize and welcome forces and energies beyond their limited selves—those of nature—recognize also that they don't create their gardens, but are partners in a co-creative act. Such gardeners have the potential to manifest gardens that are uniquely different from those created by human will alone.

"Nature Spirits"

What was once for me an unconscious response to natural forms, especially plants, has become a profound connection to and communication with nature. Through this growth, I've come to feel more attuned to cultures other than my own. In today's North American culture, I sense a general alienation from the rest of creation. This seems to be the prevailing attitude in most industrialized nations, where people at large are disconnected from such basics as food, and wherein materialistic philosophies have taken precedence over other ways of thinking. Inherent in this materialistic approach is the idea that we humans are superior to nature: that it exists to be subdued, manipulated or otherwise controlled for our own purposes. Our security is derived from attempting to gain more and more power over nature. The material mindset sees a rock as only a rock, a plant as nothing more than a plant: to believe otherwise is superstition. Yet there are many world cultures that acknowledge the living spirit essence of plants as well as that of animals, insects, birds, rocks and the elements.

Such heritages perceive as much spirit on the earth plane as in any heaven: spirit is immanent in the world, not outside of it. At the same time, realities recognized by the physical senses are only partial: the world is ultimately mysterious, and not entirely knowable, measureable or controllable. All life is sacred and we are each a sacred part of it. Physical life is a vehicle for spiritual life; no part is greater than any other because each plays its own unique and special role. People in many such cultures revere all their relations with things of the Earth and, when taking plants or animals for sustenance, communicate humbly, respectfully and thankfully with their essence—the spirit of the plant or animal.

In the past twenty years, communication with nature has become a more believable notion to so-called civilized minds. At Findhorn, in Scotland, it is claimed that, with the help of nature spirits, gardeners grew 35-pound (16-kg) cabbages in the windswept sand. The foremost organic gardener in Australia, Michael Roads, has written two best-selling books about sharing the wisdom and spirit of trees, plants, birds and earth. Similarly, in the U.S., Machaelle Wright has written eloquently about her experiences of co-creating with devas and nature spirits in her Perelandra Garden, explaining the radiance of its vegetables and flowers during times of disastrous drought in Virginia as evidence of their guidance.

These books are listed in the bibliography and make extremely provocative reading. Their thrust is clearly about rediscovering our latent and unlimited ability to communicate and unite with the energies of nature. Their messages and tone are unequivocal and perhaps never more timely. This time of global change calls for us to awake from our self-imposed isolation: to step beyond our unconscious communion with the natural world to a new level of understanding—a conscious linking with it. In such a harmonious state, we would cease from willfully treating natural forms as subservient or irrelevant to us and we could grow to heartfully recognize, greet and listen to all of nature's beings. We could imagine a garden all of whose inhabitants are truly co-creative, each enhancing the health and well-being of all.

Balance with Nature

To become a co-creative gardener means moving towards an approach that is at once more cooperative, intuitive, watchful and open-hearted. Instead of treating nature as "other," and the garden as a war zone in which to fight weeds, climate and insects, we can support nature's efforts to remain in balance and have faith that together, we will sustain ourselves.

In the summer of 1989, my friend Wolfgang appeared in my bean patch on vacation from the rice fields of Indonesia. He relayed to me an inspiring story that gives a poignant example of just such a natural balance.

The Indonesia Story

In November 1986, Indonesia became the first country in the world to curtail the use of pesticides and introduce a national agricultural policy of integrated pest management, that calls for working with, instead of against, natural insect cycles.

In the vast majority of Asian paddies, the brown planthopper had always been kept under biological control by indigenous predators such as spiders. Farmers were unaware of the means by which this balance was maintained, for it required no human interference. However, with the introduction and indiscriminate use of insecticides through the late '60s and '70s, the population of spiders was decimated while the brown planthopper thrived and became a very serious pest. In Indonesia, as in almost all other parts of the world, the farmers' fear, combined with pressure from multinational corporations, resulted in their using increasingly higher dosages of insecticides in order to combat the problem. This translated into greater and greater infestations of planthoppers and the destruction of millions of tons of rice. Not only were the planthoppers' natural enemies being killed off, but the pesticides were actually stimulating the reproduction of the dreaded pest. Fortunately, some courageous and knowledgeable agricultural-ists averted calamity by calling a poison a poison and by recognizing an ally in an insect. These scientists established an elaborate training network to educate farmers about the natural insect cycles that allowed their time-honored growing methods to be successful. This resulted in a complete change-about in Indonesian rice-growing policy.

Rice growers are now trained to assess and monitor the balance of field populations of both pests and predators. Pesticides are not applied if pests are being held in check. In three years, pesticide applications were reduced by close to 90 percent and yields increased by over 20 percent. Needless to say, Indonesian rice farmers are overjoyed to know that predators can control pests naturally. Their intimacy with their sacred crop has been further deepened by a new level of participation in its life.

A thought-provoking part of this story for me has to do with the metamorphosis of the wolf spider, chief among the planthopper's natural enemies. "Wolf" is the European-originated name for this particular insect. Wolves do not exist in Indonesia, but tigers do, and they occupy a special place of reverence in Indonesian mythology. A stroke of genius transformed the "wolf" spider into the "tiger" spider. A mammoth, media-based publicity campaign alerted Indonesians to the existence, significance and virtues of the newly baptised tiger spider. Monitoring population levels of the tiger spider became for rice growers a sacred activity, commensurate with rice growing itself.

This story from Indonesia is a shining example, and the first on a national scale, of honoring anew an ecological balance that was inherently sustainable before profiteers decided to "fix" it. It illustrates the need at this time to rekindle our appreciation and reverence for what already exists. We can continue to blame nature for crop failures due to weather, disease or pests or we can bow to natural cycles and honor and participate in the interplay that is life. We can go on destroying ourselves with our present attitudes to the natural world and our methods of food growing and consumption or we can commit ourselves to regenerative and sustainable ways of being on this planet.

A Matter of Survival

Hopefully Indonesia's example will encourage other governments to initiate sustainable agricultural policies. But that's something we cannot count on, given the perennial alignment of political and economic powers. And the times in which we live are unprecedented and demand very rapid change in the ways we inhabit this planet. Our awareness is quickly catching up to the fact that the medium that has always borne our human endeavors—Earth—can no longer do so. In the past 50 years, Earth has passed from a nature-dominant planet to a human-dominant one. In that same time, the abundance of nature and its ability to accomodate human needs has been so diminished and all our support systems have been so overtaxed that our very survival is threatened.

Clearly, we must reverse the domination of the thoughts and values that have brought us to this place. We have somehow to change our linear thinking, our self-imposed constraints of time and our desire for instant gratification, all of which lead us to spend so much energy and most of our time looking for more space and resources to exploit. We should throw out the Darwinian model of "survival of the fittest" that measures evolution by a linear progression, with humans as the highest form at the top of the hierarchy. We have to cease focussing so narrowly on the products of the world that we destroy the processes that produce them. We must end the careless treatment of nature that occurs so long as life is perceived as outside and apart from ourselves.

We must regenerate and restore the spaces and renewable resources we still have. By stepping outside of ourselves and working for the welfare of the whole, we can replace Darwin's model of intense competition with a truer view of continual cooperation, strong interaction and mutual dependence among life forms.

Social or Community Gardens

Land still available in urban and suburban areas can be utilized for food growing to a much greater extent than is presently done.

In the first and second World Wars, many people who were left at home facing reduced availability of food proudly joined together to create what were called "Liberty" and "Victory" gardens. Today most North American cities, following the European model, have what are called "allotment" gardens. These municipally-organized plots of land enable people who otherwise would not have access to a patch of earth to grow fruit and vegetables in the midst of a city or town. Such examples of "social" gardens are testaments to what is possible when there is a strong need or desire to grow food. These precarious times seem to me to necessitate new ways of sharing energy and resources to fulfill needs locally.

Whether in the city or country, I'm always amazed at the abundance of food that can be grown in small spaces. Even an outside patio or apartment balcony can be the site of substantial growing endeavors. The foods described in this book, however, are most efficiently grown with friends and neighbors in gardens that are at least large enough to plant a packet of beans or corn. This is how I've been fortunate to grow my gardens for the last few years. This is the direction my own food growing has been taking and I know of many other families who are combining energies in similar ways. It is so easy and enjoyable to hoe, weed and harvest the likes of beans, quinoa and amaranth with other enthusiasts. It is also very special to share the exquisite and substantial nourishment of meals made with these foods.

A way to grow high protein crops in urban settings would be to expand the concept of allotment gardens with their small family plots to include common areas that could be managed by more people. Such a pooling of space would also make it more practical to maintain soil fertility and tilth with green manures and cover crops.

Cooperative approaches can also work well in suburban areas. Church groups can convert some open ground to food-production. Families having extra space can share some with neighbors who don't. Adjacent families, both with backyard gardens, could alternate food and cover crops yearly. One rototiller and one chipper/shredder could serve all the people on a suburban block. Community compost piles could provide useable compost more quickly than individual ones because of their greater volume.

Whenever people join together for a common purpose it means that the weight of the project rests on no one person's shoulders. Whether in city or country, community gardens invite people to pitch in with their best skills and to nurture each other as well as the garden.

Beyond the Garden: Bioregionalism

Greening the Garden is written as a gardening book and, for the most part, I've kept to topics and issues relating to food and the growing of it. I also contend that widespread adoption of the crops and growing methods I describe would bring about profound social, economic and political changes. It's difficult to envision a North American diet consisting mostly of plant foods grown in ways that maintain a healthy, balanced environment. I hope I've shown that such a vision is both realistic and exciting. As already stated, I think that green gardens will inspire larger possibilities. Indeed, what is needed, and soon, is for towns, cities and geographical areas to take care of their food needs in a similar fashion. It is crucial to end our reliance on the top-down, capital-intensive agribusiness that perpetuates environmental destruction and human alienation from nature. Strategies that are imposed on agricultural land from an office thousands of miles away cannot take into account local conditions and requirements. What is essential is an approach that attempts to understand the uniqueness of natural systems while forming a community with them. We need to shape human cultural behavior to join with nature rather than to dominate and exploit it. Such an approach, philosophy, movement, attitude and practice goes by the name of *bioregionalism*.

While bioregionalism may sound like yet another "*ism*," it's been the easiest one ever for me to get used to and use. *Bio* has the same meaning of "life" as in biology (and as in the French word *biologique* which is the equivalent of our *organic*). The intent of bioregionalists is to ground human cultures within natural regions, to encourage personal intimacy with specific geographic locales or territories, in order to fit human behavior to the Earth rather than assume we can subdue the external world and get away with it.

The subject matter of this book—growing and foraging appropriate foods while honoring the sustainability of natural systems—is bioregional at heart. But bioregionalism takes the essential paradigm of a participatory interaction with nature and applies it to all the physical, psychological and spiritual ways we interact with our living place and the beings within it. Bioregionalism aims to restore and regenerate human rights, potential and dignity as well as watersheds, farms, and forests.

It is beyond the scope of *Greening the Garden* to pursue more broadly the greening of our hearts and homes. In terms of sustainable agriculture, bioregionalism honors the diversity of crops and strategies appropriate to different ecosystems. Bioregionalism extends the quality of cooperation and mutual benefit enjoyed by the "green" gardener and garden to larger ecological systems. Yet the beauty and sanity of bioregionalism is its notion of operating within bounds that are both human and natural in scale. It incorporates a sense of containment and benign limitation beyond which solutions are too imposed, too large, too generalized, too insensitive and too inefficent. In its essence, bioregionalism is about taking care of home. By keeping our own patch of earth green, and respecting others' rights to do the same, we may once again have an Earth we are proud to call Home.

Co-creating the Garden

I would like to conclude this chapter with an example of one of those surprises that can occur in a co-creative garden.

Despite growing dry beans for many years, I have yet to notice any genetic crosses that have occurred between varieties. In 1986 however, I found a genetic mutation or "sport" in an isolated patch of Montezuma Red beans. One plant had beans that were black instead of red. I saved all the "Montezuma Blacks" and each year thereafter I selected beans from their progeny that were also black, to see if I could stabilize a new variety. By harvest time in 1989, only 10 percent of the beans were red, reddish brown or grey, and the rest were black. In 1990, however, I decided to plant some of the non-black Montezumas. Not only did they produce the familiar non-black beans, but other colors and shapes, as well as mottled designs, amazed me as I opened the bean pods. Some of these bore no resemblance to any of the 120 other bean varieties I was growing.

It seemed to me as if a door had opened with the first black Montezuma plant and that I at first chose to explore but one room of a multi-storied mansion. Any of those "aberrent" beans could be doors of rooms or of passageways to more doors. I won't know the full dimensions until I knock on specific doors with the desire to find out what is there.

What this says to me is that the lifeforms that are rapidly disappearing on this planet may not be irretrievably lost. Varieties are unique combinations of the energy blueprints that science calls genes. It is possible that genes of an extinct variety still exist in another variety, though not in that particular combination. It is crucial to preserve what varieties we have left.

Nature's doors are only locked from the outside. We are the keys. And if we remember to knock with humility before entering, we may find that the Welcome mat has been there all along.

The gardening techniques and the crops described in this book are not new; they have been around for thousands of years and can be refined and adapted to farm and garden, individual and group, city, town and country. The environmental crisis we now face provides an unprecedented opportunity to rededicate ourselves to sustainability and to co-create a planet where food is once again clean and water is pure. Ways of growing that can keep our Garden green are waiting for our participation.

Bibliography

This book doesn't have a standard bibliography because my primary sources of information have been seed catalogues, radio programs, gardening magazines, personal correspondence and my own journals! Over the years I have assembled and amalgamated gleanings and snippets from all of the above into files on various subjects. When certain facts were absorbed with sufficient thoroughness, the references became less important.

I find it most appropriate, if somewhat unorthodox, to first list my favorite seed companies.

Seed Companies and Seed Exchanges

Seed catalogues are crucial sources of information and inspiration for me. I appreciate some of them far more than books for their wealth of detailed yet concise gardening lore. Seeds, themselves, are living books that tell their own marvellous stories as they grow and reproduce themselves. I look forward to receiving the catalogues of the following seed companies each new gardening year.

Canadian Seed Companies

William Dam Seeds
P.O. Box 8400, Dundas, Ontario L9H 6M1

Dominion Seed House
Georgetown, Ontario L7G 4A2

Stokes Seeds Ltd.
39 James St., Box 10, St. Catharines, Ontario L2R 6R6

Jim Ternier
Box 118, Cochin, Saskatchewan S0M 0L0

Territorial Seeds Ltd.
P.O. Box 46225, Station G, Vancouver, British Columbia V6R 4G5
(3760 West 10th Ave.)

Vesey's Seeds Ltd.
York, Prince Edward Island C0A 1P0

U.S. Seed Companies

Abundant Life Seed Foundation
P.O. Box 772, Port Townsend, Washington 98368

Seeds Blum
Idaho City Stage, Boise, Idaho 83706

Bountiful Gardens
19550 Walker Road, Willits, California 95490
(. . . deserves a special mention for their seeds, publications and efforts to grow food sustainably without draining the resources of any area)

Garden City Seeds
1324 Red Crow Road, Victor, Montana 59875-9713

J.L. Hudson, Seedsman
P.O. Box 1058, Redwood City, California 94064

Johnny's Selected Seeds
305 Foss Hill Road, Albion, Maine 04910

Mountain Meadow Farm
826 Ulrich Road, Prospect, Oregon 97536
(. . . has an excellent selection of garlic for U.S. growers)

Native Seed/Search
3950 West New York Drive, Tucson, Arizona 85745

Shepherd's Garden Seeds
30 Irene Street, Torrington, Connecticut 06790

Territorial Seeds Ltd.
P.O. Box 27, Loraine, Oregon 97451

Seed Exchanges

The seed exchanges in the U.S. and Canada are sources of seeds otherwise unobtainable. Their publications are sources of otherwise unobtainable information as to what is happening at the grass roots level in North America and elsewhere.

Heritage Seed Program
    R.R. 3, Uxbridge, Ontario L0C 1K0

Seed Savers Exchange
    R.R. 3, Box 239, Decorah, Iowa 52101

The Grain Exchange
    2440 East Water Well Rd., Salina, Kansas 67401

Seeds for crops described in this book are available from my own company and I am always happy to answer gardening correspondence.

Salt Spring Seeds
    Box 33, Ganges, British Columbia V0S 1E0

Magazines and Periodicals

I have drawn on magazines and periodicals for every chapter of the book. One in particular deserves special mention. I have learned so much from *Organic Gardening* magazine over the years that it would be a huge task to credit all its articles. *Organic Gardening*, under the leadership of Robert Rodale and his father J.I. Rodale, has been articulating the promise of sustainable, poison-free gardens and farms since 1942. Robert Rodale's untimely death in 1990 has left thousands of people more ardently following his lead in seeking ways to heal this world grown self-destructive. The Rodale Institute has published dozens of books on organic gardening but my recommendation would be to purchase a subscription to the magazine:

Organic Gardening,
> Emmaus, Pennsylvania, 18099

As with the seed companies, there are many more excellent publications than those listed. The following are my personal favorites and the ones that have contributed most to *Greening the Garden.*

> *Cognition—The Voice of Canadian Organic Growers*
> Box 6408, Station J, Ottawa, Ontario K2A 3Y6

> *Harrowsmith*
> Camden East, Ontario K0K 1J0
> or
> The Creamery, Charlotte, Vermont 05445

> *The Island Grower*
> R.R. 4, Sooke, British Columbia V0S 1N0

> *Rural Delivery*
> P.O. Box 1509, Liverpool, Nova Scotia B0T 1K0

> *Horticulture*
> P.O. Box 2592, Boulder, Colorado 80321

> *Hort Ideas*
> Route 1, Gravel Switch, Kentucky 40328

> *Henry Doubleday Research Association*
> Ryton-on-Dunsmore, Coventry, England CV8 3LG

Books

I am going to resist the urge to list many fine gardening books and instead just note the few books that were significant reference material for each section of *Greening the Garden.*

Part One

The best and most up-to-date discussion of organic gardening principles and techniques is one which especially addresses small-scale, low-impact farming. I am particularly indebted to Coleman's treatment of crop rotations and intercropping.

> *The New Organic Grower: A Master's Manual of Tools and Techniques for the Home and Market Gardener,* by Eliot Coleman
> Old Bridge Press, 1989

A classic book, written 50 years ago, still is one of the best books on soil and the processes which take part in it.

> *An Agricultural Testament,* by Sir Albert Howard
> Oxford University Press, 1943

My greatest sources by far, for ideas and information for Part One have been *Organic Gardening* Magazine and the *Henry Doubleday Research Magazine.*

Part Two

Most of the cultural information on the plants in this section comes from my own experience. Background information came largely from personal correspondence as well as magazine and newspaper articles. Athough there are recent books on quinoa and amaranth, I have not seen them.

The following two books have wonderful recipes and great information on the history, classification and preparation of legumes.

> *The Brilliant Bean,* by Sally and Martin Stone
> Bantam, 1988

> *Bean Feast,* by Valerie Turvey
> 101 Productions, 1979

The following three books are among the widest-ranging and most informative general gardening books available even though they were written for somewhat select readers—namely the English, the northern and the coastal gardener.

The Complete Food Garden, by John Seymour
Fontana, 1980

The Harrowsmith Northern Gardener, by Jennifer Bennett
Camden House, 1982

Growing Vegetables West of the Cascades, by Steve Solomon
Sasquatch Books, 1989

An organization I discovered after completing this book has been researching and popularizing fava beans for almost a decade.

The Aprovecho Institute
80574 Hazelton Road, Cottage Grove, Oregon 97424

The best introduction I know to the use of herbs for healing is a readily available paperback. I urge novices to get help from local herbalists for certain identification of plants. Although I have written two books on edible and medicinal wild plants, I have no professional authority to recommend herbs.

The Way of Herbs, by Michael Tierra
Washington Square Press, 1983

The best selection of mail-order gardening books I've seen is listed by Keith Crotz.

The American Botanist
1103 W. Truitt Ave., Chilicothe, Illinois 61523

The most prominent organization promoting the development of food production systems based on ecological principles is in Ste-Anne de Bellevue, Quebec and is under the direction of Dr. Stuart B. Hill.

Ecological Agriculture Projects
P.O. Box 191, Macdonald College, 21- 111 Lakeshore Road, Ste-Anne de Bellevue, Québec H9X 1C0

Part Three

The chapter on seed politics owes much to the work of Pat Mooney and Cary Fowler and their various writings on the subject over many years. They have recently combined their efforts and distilled their work of the past decade in the following book, which can be obtained from RAFI-USA, P.O. Box 655, Pittsboro, NC 27312, U.S.A.

> *Shattering: Food, Politics, and the Loss of Genetic Diversity*, by Cary Fowler and Pat Mooney
> University of Arizona Press, 1990

The chapter on saving seed drew most on editions of the above listed Seed Savers Exchange. In 1991, they put out the definitive book on the subject.

> *Seed to Seed*, by Suzanne Ashworth
> Seed Savers Exchange, 1991

The chapter on food choices was greatly influenced by John Robbins' *Diet for a New America*. Many of the statistics in this chapter are direct quotes from this Pulitzer Prize-nominated work. It is a must-read book for anyone interested in how food choices affect personal and planetary health.

> *Diet for a New America,* by John Robbins
> Stillpoint Publishing, 1987

Robbins himself, as did I, relied considerably on the work of Frances Moore Lappé, mentioned in my introduction to Part Two.

Diet for a Small Planet, by Frances Moore Lappé
   Ballantine, 1982

As background to the last chapter on Co-creating the Garden, the following three books are about sharing the energies and spirit of plants, animals, birds, insects and earth.

The Perelandra Garden Workbook, by Machaelle Small Wright
   Perelandra, 1987

The Findhorn Gardern
   Findhorn Community, 1975

Talking With Nature, by Michael J. Roads
   Kramer, 1987

I don't think you'll find more erudite or cogent arguments for our need to reconnect with nature than in the writings of Wendell Berry or Thomas Berry.

The Unsettling of America: Culture and Agriculture, by Wendell Berry
   Sierra Club Books, 1977

The Dream of the Earth, by Thomas Berry
   Sierra Club Books, 1988

And for more on bioregionalism, the subtitle of the following book says it well: "An exciting vision and strategy for creating ecologically sustainable communities and cultures in harmony with the limits and regenerative powers of the Earth:"

Home! A Bioregional Reader, edited by Van Andruss, Christopher Plant, Judith Plant and Eleanor Wright
   New Society Publishers, 1990

Index

A

Abundant Life Seed
Foundation 54, 59
actinomycetes 16
adzuki beans 40
alfalfa 18, 23, 24
algae 16
allantoin 115
allicin 94
amaranth 53, 63–66, 157
amino 53
amino acids 53
anaerobic decomposition 16
annual plants 152, 153
aphids 43, 76
asparagus 90, 121

B

bacteria 16, 23, 27, 42. *See
also* microorganisms
bark 31
barley 25, 28
basil 126–127
beans 23, 29, 37
beetles 43
beets 28, 122, 135, 158
bell bean 77
Berberis. See Oregon grape
biennial plants 152, 153
bioregionalism 140, 180-181
BLACK BEAN THANKSGIVING 48
BLACK SOY EXPRESS 47
blight 30, 43
bloodmeal 9, 12, 26

bonemeal 9, 12, 42
boneset. *See* comfrey
brassicas 120, 132–
134, 160, 162
broad bean 77
broccoli 120, 132, 160
Brundtland Commission 3
Brussels
sprouts 120, 129, 133,
160, 162
buckwheat 25
burdock 98–99, 107
bush beans 40

C

cabbage 28, 90, 120, 133,
152, 160, 162
cabbage root fly 9, 131
calcium 8, 16, 25
carbon 17, 26
cardboard 32
carrot 28, 31, 122, 135, 159
carrot rust fly 131
cauliflower 29, 120, 133,
160, 162
celeriac 136
celery 120, 124, 134
chard 121
chervil 136
chick-peas 25, 39, 79–80
chickweed 97–98
chicory 103, 107
Chinese mustards 129
Chinese spinach 65